The Twentieth-Century Novel:
An Introduction

The Twentieth-Century Novel:
An Introduction

R. B. Kershner

University of Florida

BEDFORD BOOKS BOSTON ≈ NEW YORK

For Richard Brandon Kershner, M. Amanda Kershner,
and James W. Kershner

For Bedford Books
President and Publisher: Charles H. Christensen
General Manager and Associate Publisher: Joan E. Feinberg
Managing Editor: Elizabeth M. Schaaf
Developmental Editor: Stephen A. Scipione
Editorial Assistant: Rebecca Jerman
Production Editor: Bridget Leahy
Copyeditor: Barbara G. Flanagan
Cover Design: Ann Gallager

Library of Congress Catalog Card Number: 96–86773

Manufactured in the United States of America.

1 0 9 8 7
f e d c b a

For information, write: Bedford Books, 75 Arlington Street, Boston, MA 02116
(617-426-7440)

ISBN: 0–312–10244–5 (paperback)
ISBN: 0–312–16376–2 (hardcover)

Published and distributed outside North America by:

MACMILLAN PRESS LTD.
Houndmills, Basingstoke, Hampshire RG21 2XS and London Companies
and representatives throughout the world.

ISBN: 0–333–69095–8

American empirical tradition, Van Ghent claims, "the subject matter of novels is human relationships in which are shown the directions of men's souls." Novels individualize, where history is collective. Van Ghent's interest in Gestalt psychology leads to her vision of the novel as a psychologically convincing "world"; good novels have "integral structure" and also have individual character, and each is judged by "the cogency and illuminative quality of the view of life that it affords."[6]

In British academic life, criticism took a somewhat different turn, largely because of the school gathered around F. R. Leavis. Leavis, who taught at Cambridge University between 1927 and 1964, edited *Scrutiny* magazine from 1932 to 1953; the approach promulgated by him and his wife, Queenie (Roth) Leavis gathered many enthusiastic converts to the new and newly significant field of English studies. The Leavises stressed the importance of rigorous critical analysis, especially by means of "close reading," an unremitting attention to the complexities of the text. Their conviction was that the creative energies unleashed in great literature are the same as those necessary for a fulfilling life — and are imperiled by modern, barbarically commercial civilization. One's judgment of literature is intertwined with one's vision of modern civilization as a whole. In outline if not in detail these convictions mirrored those of D. H. Lawrence, one of F. R. Leavis's literary heroes. The Leavises shared T. S. Eliot's vision of a lost sensibility uniting the intellectual and the sensual, which became fragmented sometime around the seventeenth century; they also shared his and Lawrence's belief that the twentieth century was a period of slackening standards, encroaching commercialization, and increasing mechanism, haunted by the lack of spiritual faith and by the loss of an "organic," agrarian, unified human experience.

According to F. R. Leavis's *Great Tradition* (1948), the great novelists are Jane Austen, George Eliot, Henry James, Joseph Conrad, and D. H. Lawrence; Dickens, originally excluded, was later included. Banished from the central canon were not only Richardson, Fielding, and most of the Victorians, but Woolf and Joyce — who, however, almost always overshadowed Lawrence in the opinion of American academics. Where to his followers Leavis's judgments were seen as the inevitable result of rigorous standards applied to key passages of great writers, to a later generation they often seemed more the result of personal prejudices justified after the fact. Leavis's favorite authors tended to be politically conservative; whether this is significant or not, it adds to the irony that Leavis's major successor was the politically committed leftist Raymond Williams.

Williams, who also taught at Cambridge, in works such as *Culture and Society* (1958) and *The Long Revolution* (1961) launches an argument he called the "design" of a work, but Forster gives new prominence to metaphors that are spatial rather than temporal, those that invoke an idea of the novel as a unified aesthetic whole all of which exists simultaneously.

The Rise of Criticism

In somewhat different ways in England and in America, professional literary critics began to survey and to formalize ideas about the novel. Already in 1927 Forster felt he must apologize for the fact that he was not a scholar, as he delivered the university lectures that became *Aspects of the Novel*. But the very fact that professional scholars were writing seriously about the novel lent the form increased credibility. In America the first important such work was Percy Lubbock's *The Craft of Fiction* (1921). Lubbock codifies several of James's ideas about the novel, especially his stress on point of view and his psychological emphasis; the kind of criticism that descended from Lubbock has been described as "more Jamesian than James." Form and unity, which James discusses with a craftsman's interest, Lubbock portrays as all-important.

As the ideas adumbrated by Lubbock and by Joseph Warren Beach in *The Twentieth Century Novel: Studies in Technique* (1932) became widely accepted among academics, they created the implicit assumption that the evolution of the novel had been a progressive movement toward late-nineteenth-century social realism and that the novel's main purpose was the nuanced exploration of psychology within that context. Further, special value was attached to formal manipulations of the novel's elements, so that (for example) Conrad's play with chronology was seen as admirable, while the stream-of-consciousness technique of Woolf, Joyce, and Faulkner garnered praise on both formal and psychological grounds. In general, novels that worked like poems (such as the modern "art novel") gained ground, and "loose, baggy monsters" (however wide-ranging or well documented) lost it. The culmination of the Jamesian tradition in novel criticism was probably Leon Edel's *The Modern Psychological Novel* (1955).

Most Jamesian notions adapted well to the critical doctrine called the "New Criticism" which held sway from about the 1930s until the 1960s in America; Caroline Gordon and Allen Tate, two well-known New Critics, in *The House of Fiction* (1950) formalized the relationship. For generations of students, Cleanth Brooks and Robert Penn Warren's *Understanding Fiction* (1943) served as a basic text. A looser use of New Critical approaches was made by Dorothy Van Ghent in her popular *English Novel: Form and Function* (1953). Coming out of the Anglo-

Preface

I have taught courses in the twentieth-century novel—both British and American—for more than twenty years, and each time I teach such a course it seems clear to me that along with discussions of the particular novels we read in class I need to present some information about the novel itself—what a novel is, how the form developed before the twentieth century, how writers and critics have thought about the novel, and so forth. In addition, in a course concentrating on twentieth-century writing I find it very useful if my students are acquainted with the broad outlines of the development of literature over the past century—the schools, movements, trends, and countertrends not only in literature but in the other arts as well. As soon as we start to discuss any single novel in detail, I also find it necessary to present some of the technical terminology and the concepts through which critics approach problems of plot, character, setting, and point of view. It seemed to me that it would be helpful if there were a source containing all this information to which I could send students.

My hope is that by assigning *The Twentieth-Century Novel: An Introduction* early in their courses, instructors will free themselves to spend more class time on the particular novels they are studying and on the themes they want to develop. So far as I am aware, this is the only survey of the twentieth-century novel written for college students.

In the first chapter I outline key issues in and approaches to the novel, and in the second I concentrate on the rise of modernism as a literary movement within the broader cultural context of modernity. The third chapter presents a sketch of modern literary history and emphasizes the rise of postmodernism in the novel. Probably the cultural events with the greatest impact on literary study over that period, aside from the recognition of postmodernism, are the rise of ethnic and postcolonial studies and the development of gender criticism, including feminism and, most recently, "queer theory." These events, treated in the fourth and fifth chapters, not only have provided us with a new and challenging set of questions through which to address literature and a much larger list of texts to examine but also have altered some of the basic assumptions within which, thirty years ago, most British and American literary critics plied their trade.

In the glossary I have included a more rigorous discussion of what might be called "fundamentals" of the novel, including the issues dealt with by "narratologists." In addition, the wealth of literary and critical terms introduced and defined throughout the book can be located through the index. As a whole, this book is a brief supplement that would be helpful in any course in twentieth-century fiction in English, whether British, American, or multicultural. It would be entirely appropriate for courses in the novel as a genre and should be useful for courses in contemporary fiction as well as for those that concentrate on the modernist period. Instructors, of course, may choose to assign certain sections and not others. I might add that although undergraduates are the primary intended audience of *The Twentieth-Century Novel: An Introduction*, my own graduate students have found it useful. Indeed, I personally learned a great deal writing this book, and I hope that despite its introductory nature my colleagues will find parts of it illuminating.

Students come to courses in the modern novel with strikingly different kinds of preparation, even more so today than formerly. Some will have read Richard Wright and Zora Neale Hurston but not Hawthorne or Melville; some the reverse. A surprising number are unclear on the difference between "literature" and "novels." In my experience, an instructor can never take for granted what undergraduate students "should know"; but I am forever being confronted by the amazing and delightful variety of things they *do* know that I didn't. In writing this book I have tried to assume nothing about the knowledge students bring to their courses. I have defined terms as I use them, and added a brief explanation of references I make to literary works. At the same time, I have avoided "dumbing down" any of the discussions. Some of the issues in contemporary literary theory, which is often packed with technical terminology and difficult concepts, are presented here in simplified and abbreviated form; but at the same time I have done my best to give an idea of the richness and complexity of, for instance, feminist theory. For students who would like to pursue a subject in more depth or detail, I have provided a short annotated bibliography of each area I discuss.

Acknowledgments

I have a great many people to thank for inspiring and aiding this project, beginning with Charles H. Christensen, publisher of Bedford Books, who suggested to me some four years ago that a book like this might be useful. After him, I probably owe the most to Daniel Cottom, who suggested that I write something along the lines of the last three chapters. That would be the part of the book most likely to interest *him,* he observed, leaving me with the inference that I should produce a book accessible to most undergraduates on the one hand and interesting to an expert in literary theory on the other. I can only hope that my efforts have resulted in a book that has something to offer both groups.

My colleagues at the University of Florida have been remarkably patient with my continual requests for book lists and information in their various specialties, though none of course is responsible for my omissions and errors. I want to thank Robert Thomson, John van Hook, Anne Goodwyn Jones, Elizabeth Langland, Alistair Duckworth, Brian McCrea, Carl Bredahl, David Leverenz, John Murchek, Stephanie Smith, Marsha Bryant, Mildred Hill-Lubin, Mark Reid, Malini Schueller, Phillip Wegner, and Susan Hegeman for help. Kim Emery, Robert Ray, and Amitava Kumar carefully critiqued early drafts of chapters for me, and each of them saved me from saying a number of things I did not in fact mean. John Seelye kindly made available the help of his research assistant, Wim de Groote of the University of Antwerp. Among the graduate students, Leslie Henson and Bonnie Tensen were particularly helpful with books and advice, as was my former student and present colleague Monica Ayuso de Ventimiglia. Another former student and present colleague, M. Keith Booker, helped greatly with his encyclopedic knowledge of the modern novel. Brian Richardson of the University of Maryland was generous with his expertise in the study of narration. I greatly appreciate the helpful and perceptive comments of the publisher's reviewers: Kent Bales, Mary Jean Corbett, Patrick O'Donnell, James Phelan, David H. Richter, Ellen Rooney, Herbert Sussman, and Kari J. Winter. I want to thank the graduate and undergraduate classes in modern literature that I have taught over the past few years for allowing me to "road-test" some of the material in this book and, in some cases, for usefully suggesting changes in it.

For a semester during the writing of this book I taught on exchange at the University of Utrecht in the Netherlands, and I owe my colleagues there for many courtesies. I especially want to thank Prof. Dr. Peter de Voogd, chair of the department of English, as well as Dr. Erik Kooper, Dr. Ton Hoenselaars, and Dr. Paul Franssen. Prof. Dr. Hans Bertens, chair of American studies, has been a good friend for many years, and my chapter on postmodernism was greatly influenced by his book *The Idea of the Postmodern.*

As always, the staff of Bedford Books has been not only expert and professional but friendly and personally supportive; my own work on this project has had its vicissitudes, but dealing with my publishers has always been a pleasure. I wish to thank Joan Feinberg, Elizabeth Schaaf, Laura Arcari, Mark Reimold, Rebecca Jerman, Barbara Flanagan, and Janet Cocker. I especially want to thank Bridget Leahy, my production editor, and Steve Scipione, who was always ready with an encouraging word when I needed one.

Contents

Theories of the Novel

So pervasive is the novel in Western society today that many people tend to confuse "novel" with "fiction" or even with "literature." In fact, the novel is just one form fiction can take — the short story is another, and, technically speaking, epics and plays are fiction as well. Literature as a whole takes in a multitude of genres (or forms), such as lyric poems, tragic plays, odes, and so forth; the novel is only one such genre and a relatively recent one at that (see the discussion under *novel* in the glossary at the end of this book).

It is sometimes a surprise to modern readers that the novel was under attack for much of its history, but in the view of the Roman Catholic Church — and of many Protestant sects as well — novels were frivolous entertainment that distracted readers from proper concentration on their spiritual state. The fundamental characteristic that distinguishes the novel from most Western literature that preceded it — its appeal to the reader's daily experience — is what made it difficult to defend against these charges of triviality and pernicious worldliness. Meanwhile, the fact that the novel is fiction (that is, an elaborate and sustained falsehood) made it difficult to defend on the grounds that it might teach something useful. Even today there are remnants of this attitude; the novelist Harry Crews says that his mother has never really understood the fact that he earns his living telling stories "that aren't even true."

How the novel was seen by society in a given period, or indeed whether novel-like writing was recognized at all, depended greatly on the social, religious, moral, and political assumptions of the audience — what, broadly speaking, we could call its ideology. For the novel, it is very likely that technology was of fundamental importance as well. Before the invention of movable type around 1450, which brought the possibility of rapid, large print runs, it is unlikely that writing as long and elaborately detailed as novels could have reached any sort of audience. Epic poems were long but were composed metrically, allowing them to be memorized by professional performers. In any case, during the medieval period (roughly 500 A.D.–1500) such was the dominance of the Roman Catholic Church that most writing consisted of theological commentaries, some religious drama, lives of the saints, fables, and exempla, none of which made much use of the details of contemporary experience. And as a practical matter, readership was limited to the clergy and the nobility, both of whose daily experience was very unlike most people's.

During the Renaissance period of the sixteenth and seventeenth centuries, there was a revival of interest in some of the fictional forms practiced by the ancient Greeks and Romans, including the Symposia and Menippean satire, and historical chronicles appeared in England. Romances (courtly stories in verse) appeared in many European countries in the medieval period and in England from the thirteenth century onward — around the time we begin to find literature written in the various vernacular European languages instead of exclusively in Latin. These romances generally concern the experiences of either King Arthur's or Charlemagne's courts or those of classical heroes. The events are frequently magical or centered on love; the tone is elevated; and the moral of the story is also its point. Starting in the fifteenth century, some of these romances in England appear in prose instead of in verse.

In retrospect, we are tempted to see any prose form of narrative fiction as a precursor of the novel or an approximation to it, but we should remember that in the mid-eighteenth century — the time (as we now see it) when the novel, properly speaking, arose — both critics and the authors themselves were much more inclined to discuss these books as *histories* or *romances* than by the relatively new term *novel*. Indeed, up to the late nineteenth century some novelists still insisted that they were writing romances; only in the twentieth century did *romance* take on its current somewhat debased connotation of a sentimental love story and the word *novel* begin to be used with a positive connotation. This is partly an effect of the inherent conservatism of the arts. Creative work in the medieval period was usually financed by the Church; in the Renaissance period it tended to be sponsored by the nobility. The first people we might regard as professional writers, such as Thomas Nashe (1567–1601) and Robert Greene (1558–1592), were writing in the late sixteenth century, but for the next two hundred years it was still common practice for writers to dedicate their works to noble sponsors. It now seems apparent that a crucial factor in the rise of the novel was the appearance of a newly literate middle-class audience for literary production, yet for centuries writers continued to write with at least half an eye on pleasing the nobility and avoiding the Church's censure.

In the Renaissance period, some cultural factors were encouraging to the possibility of the novel: there was a new openness to exploration of the physical world (reflected in the popularity of travelers' tales) and a desire to verify ideas through personal experience rather than by appealing to authority. But while the Renaissance's reverence for Greek and Roman literary figures and its desire to emulate them encouraged production in the arts, it also discouraged to some extent the use of forms unknown to the ancients. Besides, while drama (such as Shakespeare's) could claim to be a genuinely popular form, literacy was too rare to allow the rise of a popular readership. By the eighteenth century, the readership was there, but critics were slow to recognize the importance of that fact; taste, it was felt, was an absolute, universal and unchanging, and the preferences of one or another nationality or class had nothing to do with the issue. Novels, after all, are not objects like trees, which are either there or not, regardless of the observer. Whether the novel exists or not is a matter of consensus, and literary consensus is slow in forming.

Samuel Johnson (1709–1784) represented the literary taste of his age, and in *Rambler* essay number 4 (1750), he has praise for the novel. But he calls it at one point the "comedy of romance," and distinguishes it from the "heroic romance" by its verisimilitude, its accuracy to life. At another point he calls it a "familiar history," and praises its ability to instill virtue and discourage vice more effectively than sermons or heroic romances, precisely because its characters and experiences are familiar to readers. But he also gravely warns that there is a potential conflict between verisimilitude and moral effectiveness — if characters are drawn with the moral ambiguity we find in real persons, then readers may well draw the wrong lesson from their adventures, or no lesson at all. Johnson saw no reason why in novels "there should not be exhibited the most perfect idea of virtue." But then Johnson, although he wrote prose fiction, was no novelist. As we shall see, each literary age — and each individual commentator — stamped the novel with a distinctive set of concerns.

THE CLASSICAL INHERITANCE

Novel means "new," and to name a literary genre or kind after the mere fact of its novelty is somewhat paradoxical — after all, literary kinds are generally thought to be traditional, and most of them descend from (and derive their authority from) classical Latin and Greek examples. The novel, which is arguably the most important genre in English literature after the mid-eighteenth century, is different. The word was derived from *novella*, an Italian term for a short tale in prose, but this derivation did not seem very important to the writers first using the English term. Critics can trace the sources of the novel back to various classical narratives and extended prose works, but most agree that before the eighteenth century, in England at least, nothing very close to the novel existed. Further, they usually contrast the novel to the earlier form of the romance. In many European languages the term for novel is *roman*, which is related to *romance*, and so implies a continuity with medieval prose works, called by that name. Literary theorists of the *roman* naturally see the entire question of the novel's position differently from theorists of the novel.

Since the classical authorities did not discuss the novel per se, eighteenth-century critics could not take the writings of Plato (c. 428–348/347 B.C.) and Aristotle (384–322 B.C.) as an immediate point of departure, as occurred with other genres. But larger issues that these early philosophers raised nevertheless tended to dominate discussions of the new form. Among these, imitation, or *mimesis*, was probably the most important concept. In book 10 of *The Republic* (c. 370 B.C.) Plato has Socrates argue that the arts in general are a distraction from the search for truth. Things of this world, Plato asserts, are only imitations of their ideal forms, and so a painting or a poem is only an imitation of an imitation. Further, poets are inclined to appeal to "the lachrymose and fitful temper" of an audience rather than to its "rational principle," since the former is easier to "imitate." This is the reason why, despite his great respect for writers like Homer, Plato decides to banish poets from his Republic. Much of the Western world's discussions about the position of the arts in a community — from eighteenth-century exchanges over whether the novel improves readers right down to current debates about funding the National Endowment for the Arts — ultimately descends from Plato.

Where Plato sees imitation as essentially a philosophical and social function that is more or less accurate and more or less beneficial, Plato's student Aristotle sees the imitative act as creative in itself. He is interested less in the social function of art and more in the analysis of art's kinds and processes. More concerned with aesthetics than is Plato, in some ways Aristotle is the first "formalist" critic — that is, he is interested in the work of art *in itself.* The form he chooses for analysis is *tragedy,* which he regards as the highest form of art. For Aristotle, imitation is characteristic of all the arts and includes means such as rhythm, tune, and meter, even in some kinds of verbal art. Imitation is always in some way imitation of nature, and just as the parts of a natural object contribute to the whole, so must the parts of a tragedy organically contribute to its unity. Further, in imitating persons, he points out, artists may show them as better, worse, or just the same as they are in actuality. Even the kind of narration through which actions are imitated may vary. Thus Aristotle vastly complicates the concept of imitation, and the aesthetic and moral consequences of this complication will occupy writers for two millennia.

In addition, a number of the concepts Aristotle developed specifically in relation to tragedy were later adapted to discussions of the novel. *Catharsis,* the purifying or purging flow of emotion experienced by the audience (by readers in the case of a novel), is one such idea that provides a means by which unpleasant representations may ultimately have a positive effect upon an audience. The *peripeteia,* or reversal, is a plot moment in tragedy often found in novels as well, and in the analysis of character the idea of *hamartia,* interpreted as "tragic flaw," is often thought useful in novels. Finally, working from some hints in Aristotle's *Poetics* (335–322 B.C.), European critics between the sixteenth and eighteenth centuries developed the "rule of the three unities" of action, time, and place. Although this rule was applied strictly only to drama, the stress on unity of effect in drama led eventually to the development of "organic" views of art, including the novel, in which stress was laid upon an overall aesthetic unity and an internal harmony of parts in the work.

THE SEVENTEENTH AND EIGHTEENTH CENTURIES

The concepts of history and romance dominated seventeenth- and eighteenth-century discussions of the prose form that would become known as the novel. Because new literary forms were often met with suspicion, writers of prose narratives tended to present and to justify their offerings to the public as either history or romance — and sometimes, paradoxically, both — for each had its own rationale. "True histories" were seen as worthwhile because of their information value, whether they were typical or unusual — and, indeed, there is still much ambiguity in our intuitive concept of the "realistic" as to whether realism is most convincingly found in what is ordinary and typical or in what is individual and unusual. In the late seventeenth century the growing public appetite for "news" extended to ballads based in fact, memoirs, biographies, and "realistic" prose narratives of lives, actual or not. For much of the eighteenth century, the word *novel* also meant "news." Aphra Behn (1640–1689) defends her early novel *Oroonoko, or the History of the Royal Slave* (1688) by distinguishing it from a romance, claiming that Oroonoko is no "feign'd Hero whose Life and Fortunes Fancy may manage at the Poet's Pleasure." In contrast, Daniel Defoe (1660–1731) asserts in the preface to *Robinson Crusoe* (1719) that Crusoe's adventures are worth reading especially because of their wonder and variety — though Defoe later has Crusoe affirm in the preface to the book's sequel that the book is no mere "romance." In the preface to *Moll Flanders* (1722) he distinguishes between Moll's "private History" (scandalous though it may be) and the recently fashionable "Novels and Romances."

But Defoe's pretended autobiographies — what he claims as "history" — are less characteristic of most of the fiction produced in the late seventeenth and early eighteenth centuries than are the "amatory novellas" of writers like Eliza Haywood (1693?–1756). These purvey mildly erotic fantasies and melodramas with little claim to inform the reader about the external facts of worldly life. But as Haywood points out in her dedication to *The Fatal Secret, or Constancy in Distress* (1724), though she as a woman has been given no formal education, as a woman she does know much about love, "that which Nature is not negligent to teach us." Because of the situation of women and the mythology surrounding them, Haywood was almost forced to this defense, but in fact with the appearance of Samuel Richardson's (1689–1761) hugely influential works, especially *Pamela* (1740–1741) and *Clarissa* (1747–1749), it could be argued that the novel's justification shifted from an informative mimesis of the political and social world to an imitation of the domestic, personal, and emotional world. The novel, it was increasingly argued, was the domain of moral and ethical truth — a potential it could fulfill as easily by stressing romance and interiority as by stressing history and the external world.

A division also arose between the types of novels produced by relatively well educated writers (such as Henry Fielding), who often had aristocratic connections, and those produced by writers without such education or social status (such as the majority of women authors and Richardson). In the preface to *Joseph Andrews* (1742), a complex, witty, and self-consciously crafted fiction, Fielding (1707–1754) calls the book both "a comic romance" and "a comic epic-poem in prose." His entertaining novels incorporate elements of comic drama, fable, and essay as well. His characters, he points out, are not so elevated as those in the "grave romance" — the heroic romances of medieval times — nor so debased as those in the popular comic "burlesque." Though in *Tom Jones* (1749) he claims to be "the founder of a new province of writing," he insists that his work is also continuous with the classical genres. In his invocation both of the epic and of the romance Fielding seems to be insisting on a broad social canvas, and many novelists following him take this to be an essential characteristic of the novel.

Richardson's novels have a far narrower canvas. For both *Pamela, or Virtue Rewarded* and *Clarissa: or The History of a Young Lady*, in their intense focus on the attempted seduction of a middle-class woman by a gentleman, depend heavily on minute particulars of experience and on the emotional and ethical adventures of the protagonists. Defensive about his relative lack of learning, Richardson attempts to justify his multivolume epistolary novel *Clarissa* as a new variety of Christian tragedy. But he also defends his practice in terms that were to become dominant in nineteenth-century theories of realism: the "necessity to be very circumstantial and minute in order to preserve and maintain that air of probability which is necessary to be maintained in a Story designed to represent real life." As for the book's inordinate length (about one million words in eight volumes), Richardson quotes one of his defenders in arguing that if the characters are "various and natural" and there is sufficient "variety of incidents," "and these so conducted, as to keep the reader always awake" then the greater the length of the narrative, the greater the reader's pleasure.

The major arbiter of late eighteenth-century taste, Samuel Johnson, was an admirer of Richardson but by no means an enthusiast of novels in general. In *Rambler* essay number 4 (1750), he describes the main audience of fiction as "the young, the ignorant, and the idle" and warns about the "power of example" of fiction, which can "take possession of the memory by a kind of violence and produce effects almost without the intervention of the will" — an argument frequently made today about television. Despite Fielding's higher social status, Johnson disapproves of his characters, who he thinks are mostly drawn from "low life." Where Richardson draws "characters of nature," Johnson told his biographer James Boswell, Fielding's are "characters only of manners." Fidelity to nature, for Johnson, is not a matter of numbering "the streaks of the tulip," as he puts it, but of representing ideal types and psychological truths that transcend the accident of a particular historical place and time. In the Preface to his edition of Shakespeare (1765) Johnson states that "nothing can please many, and please long, but just representations of general nature." For Johnson the categories of realism and idealism were interrelated in ways that seem alien to twentieth-century standards, and Richardson with his greater explicit didactic concern was the beneficiary of Johnson's orientation.

While many novelists were putting increasing stress on historicity, realism, and variety, romance was by no means dead. In *The Progress of Romance* (1785), Clara Reeve (1729–1807) distinguishes between the forms: "The Novel is a picture of real life and manners, and of the time in which it is written. The Romance, in lofty and elevated language, describes what never happened nor is likely to happen." Traditional romances (usually involving knights and ladies) continued to thrive despite being parodied by Cervantes (1547–1616) in *Don Quixote* (1605). After 1750 the Gothic novel, following Horace Walpole's (1717–1797) *Castle of Otranto* (1765), emerged with all its furniture of ghosts, vaults, living statues, and family curses. This unheroic variety of romance, which was to lead both to the modern genre of horror fiction and, via Charlotte Brontë's (1816–1855) *Jane Eyre* (1847), to what we now term the popular romance genre, had relatively few formal defenders, but many eager readers. With its stress on the fantastic, the supernatural, and the macabre, and its props of haunted castles, graveyards, and ruins, the Gothic novel made an appeal to fancy, romance, and the reader's imagination — an appeal that could not be easily justified in critical terms until the advent of romanticism, with its new literary values, in the late eighteenth and early nineteenth centuries.

THE NINETEENTH CENTURY

The novel's development during the nineteenth century is generally discussed under a rubric such as "the rise of realism," since the period saw the consolidation of fictional technique in the "mainstream realist novel." In the eyes of many critics, the century witnessed the fruition of the form in the work of Jane Austen (1775–1817) and in the best novelists of the Victorian period (1837–1901): Anthony Trollope (1815–1882), George Eliot (1819–1880), William Makepeace Thackeray (1811–1863), and Charles Dickens (1812–1870). Among non-British authors, the French novelist Honoré de Balzac (1799–1850) and the Russian Leo Tolstoy (1882–1945) were held in similar esteem by British readers. But if the novels of these authors represented a kind of consensus about realistic technique, the nineteenth century was equally marked by trends, tendencies, and schools that contested the dominance of realism. First among these was romance, which found a spokesman in the enormously popular historical novelist Sir Walter Scott. Over the course of the century several outgrowths of realism, sometimes with assumptions and goals foreign to it, emerged: the aestheticism of Gustave Flaubert (1821–1880) and Henry

James (1843–1916), which saw the novel as a complex exercise in literary craft; literary naturalism, a kind of fictionalized documentary journalism, championed by Emile Zola (1845–1902); and literary impressionism, an experimental, subjective style of narration, espoused by writers such as Joseph Conrad (1859–1924) and Ford Madox Ford (1873–1939).

The Novel and the Romance

In his "Essay on Romance" (1824) Sir Walter Scott (1771–1832) defines a romance as "a fictitious narrative . . . the interest of which turns upon marvellous and uncommon incidents," whereas in the novel "the events are accommodated to the ordinary train of human events, and the modern state of society." In his series of historical novels initiated by *Waverly* (1814) Scott actually blends elements from the romance and the realistic novel. His settings are (for Londoners of his period) exotic and removed in time, and his plots involved both amorous and political intrigue as well as physical adventure; but he uses his antiquarian skills to present substantiating detail from his characters' surroundings much as do novelists writing of their own times. Perhaps more important, he usually chooses anonymous protagonists who witness historical events; the heroes and heroines of history are present, but are relegated to the books' margins, figuratively speaking. In his preface to the Waverly novels, Scott relates how his imagination was first captured by wild tales and romances, but then, tiring of the "specious miracles of fiction," he soon began to "seek in histories, memoirs, voyages and travels . . . events nearly as wonderful as those which were the work of imagination, with the additional advantage that they were at least in a great measure true."

Many of the qualities that appealed to Scott's audience, such as his exotic natural settings, his interest in folklore, and his stress upon imaginative re-creation, appeared in the aesthetic theories of William Wordsworth (1770–1850), Samuel Taylor Coleridge (1772–1834), and Percy Bysshe Shelley (1792–1822). A more lasting value developed by the romantics was the affirmation of literature as a special and superior form of writing; eventually this idea was extended to include the novel as well as poetry. But Shelley's circle produced only one important novel: Mary Shelley's (1797–1851) *Frankenstein* (1818), the famous tale of a doomed monster and his creator. Incorporating elements of domestic romance, folk fable, Gothic horror, a sentimental humanistic outlook, and scientific speculation, the book became influential late in the century as Jules Verne (1828–1905), Edgar Allan Poe (1809–1849), and H. G. Wells (1866–1946) began developing the genre later to be known as science fiction. Scott, in contrast to Shelley, had immediate followers, who further refined his style of historical, realistic romances; among them were the American James Fenimore Cooper (1789–1851), the Frenchwoman George Sand (1804–1876), and the English Edward Bulwer-Lytton (1803–1873), Benjamin Disraeli (1804–1881), and in some ways George Eliot. Jane Austen, Scott's contemporary, represents another divergence from the mainstream of realism, but her comic marriage plots feature only the interpersonal sort of romance. Scott's review of Austen's *Emma* (1816) in the *Quarterly Review* recognizes that her domestic narrative was a different, though legitimate, variety from what he called his own "big bow-wow" strain.

For many in the nineteenth century, "romance" and "fancy" were rather loose terms. They were useful for pointing toward any sort of transcendence, toward the unusual or imaginative, toward sentiment, or even toward a greater purpose for the novelist beyond mere reportage. Harriet Beecher Stowe (1811–1896), author of *Uncle Tom's Cabin* (1852), attributes her attack on slavery to romance, which is identified with "every craving for nobler . . . being than that which closes like a prison-house around us." And indeed a number of novelists who claimed "romance" for their inspiration wrote politically efficacious novels or even served in legislatures, including Bulwer-Lytton, Disraeli, Victor Hugo (1802–1885), and Eugène Sue (1804–1857). Dickens also wished his work to spur social reform, but he saw romance mostly in the improbabilities and coincidences in which he often indulged.

One other aspect of the romance strain in the novel's development should be noted: the fact that all of the most important American novelists through the late nineteenth century wrote narratives that might as accurately be termed romances as novels.[1] Nathaniel Hawthorne (1804–1864) called most of his prose tales romances; in the preface to *The House of the Seven Gables* (1851) he observes that while novels must adhere minutely to probability, in the romance a writer must present only "the truth of the human heart," though he may do that "under circumstances . . . of the writer's own choosing or creation." In particular, he may "mingle the Marvellous." Herman Melville's (1819–1891) tales of the 1840s and 1850s, which often involve exotic adventures and shipboard settings, clearly fit the definition, in Melville's expressed desire to give "more reality than real life itself can show." So do the more financially successful works of James Fenimore Cooper, especially his Leatherstocking Tales. Several critics have suggested that the American novel was ideologically less inclined to define individuals through their social positions; American narratives were and, perhaps, still are more likely to set a man or woman against nature (or even against "society") than to examine minutely the person's social movements. This produces novels that, to a British eye, resemble romances. Melodrama, sentiment, adventure, and the Gothic are characteristic American modes; and the opposition of the city to the country and the movement toward the frontier are typical nineteenth-century American concerns in fiction.

The Novel as Art and Science

Dickens spends much of his author's preface to *Bleak House* (1853) defending some of the more unlikely events in that novel. He then concludes — perhaps as a sort of blanket defense — that in *Bleak House* "I have purposely dwelt upon the romantic side of familiar things." This is all very well so long as it works: in a review of Dickens's *Our Mutual Friend*, Henry James (1843–1916) argues that while Dickens's "fancy was lively and vigorous it accomplished great things." But "the fantastic, when the fancy is dead, is a very poor business." James finds *Bleak House* "forced."

Although he sometimes flirted with ghost tales, James — an American who lived his adult life in England and who wrote novels on the British model — was most influential as a realist. He was uninterested in the distinction between romance and novel and pointed out that the French *roman*, a term which includes both concepts, served either perfectly well. In a series of essays beginning with "The Art of Fiction" (1884) and including the introductory essays to his collected novels, James articulates his sense of the importance of the novel as an art form.

In so doing, he tries to remove the novel from the threat of simplistic evaluation as either moral instruction or light entertainment. Radically, he argues that a novel cannot express "a conscious moral purpose" — "how (a novel being a picture) [can] a picture be either moral or immoral?" "A novel," he argues, "is in its broadest definition a personal, a direct impression of life: that, to begin with, constitutes its value." James does not mean to imply any sort of unjudging relativism with this statement: he makes it clear that the particular quality of the consciousness behind a work greatly determines its value. And given the unparalleled freedom of the novel, its representation of life is potentially of great importance for our knowledge of ourselves. But "it must take itself seriously for the public to take it so," he cautions. What the novel now needs, James argues, is "a theory, a conviction, a consciousness of itself behind it."

Although he does not lay out a wholly coherent aesthetic, James throughout his writings on the novel makes a few recurrent points. One is the importance of consciousness — that of the author or, frequently, that of an observing participant narrator — as central to novels. Another is the lessened importance of action and the increased importance of character. Particularly in the prefaces to the New York edition of his novels, James repeatedly stresses the significance and subtlety of an author's use of point of view. In his preface to *What Maisie Knew* (1897), for instance, James makes it clear that once he had heard the "germ" of the story at a dinner party — a child who is treated heartlessly by parents engaged in a divorce action — his chief concern was with how the tale should be told: it could not be seen through the eyes of a thoughtless little boy, but might well be seen through a sensitive girl's consciousness — but could she understand enough about her situation? "Point of view" was to become almost a religious mantra for twentieth-century critics through midcentury. James emphasizes dramatic methods of presentation as opposed to summary — what later became known as "showing" rather than "telling" — and insists on the importance of form. Form and subject, for James, are inseparable. This is an insight in which he anticipates much of twentieth-century literary criticism.

For James, a novelist's ability can be measured by the degree to which form and subject harmonize. And few artists could compete with Gustave Flaubert (1821–1880) in this regard. In his essay on Flaubert (1902) James says, "The form is in *itself* as interesting, as active, as much of the essence of the subject as the idea, and yet so close is its fit and so inseparable its life that we catch it at no moment on any errand of its own." Flaubert would certainly have appreciated this tribute, had he been alive to read it. Although he published few comments about writing, in his voluminous correspondence he sets forth unsystematically ideas about the novel that have been tremendously influential on modern British and American — to say nothing of French — novelists.

Flaubert anticipates James's ideas about the superiority of art to conventional morality: "How stupid and false all works of the imagination are made by preoccupation with morality!" he exclaims in one letter. Art earns this moral exemption, he feels, because it aims, or should aim, at gaining "the precision of the physical sciences, by means of a pitiless method." As for the artist, he should efface himself: "Passion does not make poetry, and the more personal you are, the more feeble you will be." More than fifty years later, James Joyce has his artist-hero Stephen Dedalus memorably restate Flaubert's dictum: "The artist, like God of the creation, remains within or behind or beyond or above his handiwork, invisible, refined out of existence, indifferent, paring his fingernails."

In opposition to those who felt that an artist's subject was all-important, James defends the writer's right to his *donnée*, the germ of an idea that inspires his work. Although he recognizes that the reader's sympathies may be limited if the author chooses a subject with little appeal, James stresses that it is the execution that is of paramount importance to the work as art. Flaubert had already pushed this idea to a limit in writing to a friend, "What strikes me as beautiful, what I should like to do, is a book about nothing, a book without external attachments, which would hold together by itself through the internal force of its style." In such a novel "the subject would be almost invisible." Flaubert seems to suggest that there is something cheap about obviously striking or important subjects — such as those treated by romantic writers and painters. But apparently tawdry subjects like the amours of a bourgeois adulteress of no intellectual distinction — the subject of *Madame Bovary* (1857) — leaves room for the author to pursue perfection of style and structure. Flaubert's cult of the *mot juste,* the precisely right word that a writer can hope to find after sufficient work, helped to earn the modern novelist a cultural status that eventually would rival that of the poet.

Although Flaubert is often spoken of as the founder of literary realism, in fact some of his ideas, like the diminishing importance of subject, do not point in that direction at all, but rather to an aesthetic preoccupation with the work of art as a self-enclosed, self-sufficient entity. Flaubert's *Salammbô* (1862) is a historical fantasy, while *The Temptation of Saint Anthony* (1874) is a phantasmagoria. His unfinished *Bouvard and Pécuchet* (1881) is not obviously novelistic at all. These works were less influential on nineteenth-century fiction than they would prove to be on twentieth-century fiction; both modernist and postmodernist approaches to the novel can be traced to Flaubert's example. So, in part, can the "art for art's sake" movement of the turn of the century, which produced a few strange novels.

And perhaps more important than his writing itself was his attitude, especially his sense of alienation as an artist and his contempt for the bourgeoisie of which he was supposedly a member. Increasingly after the death of Dickens, those novelists who took their work most seriously and were most inclined to view themselves as artists also found their audiences limited; at the same time, the most popular writers were generally dismissed by writers of higher prestige but lower sales. More and more, the serious literary artist found himself or herself in a stance of opposition to social norms of the time.

One such group of literary radicals were the Naturalists. An important offshoot of the realist movement, this school was led and championed by the French writer Émile Zola (1840–1902). Zola in some respects built upon Flaubert's frequent comparisons between the novelist and the physician or the physical scientist in his insistence on objectivity, and indeed Flaubert encouraged his young follower. In a letter to Ivan Turgenev, however, Flaubert admitted that "reality, as I see it, should be a springboard," while Zola and his followers "are convinced that by itself it is the whole State. Such materialism makes me angry."

Indeed, Zola's materialism was unabashed. He declared himself a determinist, and one who believed that there are immutable laws of heredity and even of social change. In a preface to the first volume of his *Rougon-Macquart* novels (1871) Zola announces that in dealing with his characters, "taking into account the two-fold question of temperaments and environments," he will analyze the extended family as a social group and then "show this group in action, as the actor of an historical era." In his essay "The Experimental Novel" (1880) Zola claims to base his novelistic method on the physician Claude Bernard's *Introduction to the Study of Experimental Medicine*, which presents the physician as observer and as experimenter. This, he asserts, is exactly the role of the naturalistic novelist, who sets his characters in motion in a milieu he has studied carefully and then observes their actions. With a bow to Charles Darwin, Zola mentions the importance of heredity and environment and insists upon the novelist's objectivity: "The experimental novelist is therefore he who accepts proved facts, who shows in man and society the mechanism of the phenomena which science has mastered," and who tries to suppress any personal sentiment.

Zola's refusal to affirm piously conventional spiritual, moral, and social values gave him a certain notoriety, but his writings were seen as particularly scandalous because they frankly portrayed prostitutes, factory workers, and agricultural workers in all their vulgarity — just as Flaubert's *Madame Bovary* had outraged the bourgeoisie as a tale of bourgeois adultery that was devoid of overt moralizing. Although his literary theories did not explicitly address the issue of class, Zola's method seemed much more convincing when applied to lower-class protagonists. These could more easily be "objectified" as objects of "scientific" study (in Zola's words, "human animals, nothing more") than could upper-middle-class figures like Zola himself — or most of his readers. In addition to Zola's followers in France, the most important of whom was Guy de Maupassant (1850–1893), British writers such as George Gissing (1857–1903) and Thomas Hardy (1840–1928), and Americans such as Stephen Crane (1871–1900), Frank Norris (1870–1902), and Theodore Dreiser (1871–1945) all showed the influence of naturalism. As a combination of painstaking journalistic descriptive techniques, base subject matter, and a deterministic, pseudo-scientific approach that portrays human subjects as the helpless victims of heredity and environment, naturalism in its pure form had a limited success. But some of the basic documents of literary modernism, such as the short stories of James Joyce and of Ernest Hemingway (1899–1961), could not have been written without it.

A very different sense of the novelist's mission is apparent in literary impressionism. When James in "The Art of Fiction" describes the novel as "a personal, a direct impression of life," he suggests an alternative to the putative objectivity of naturalism. "The deepest quality of the work of art," he continues "will always be the quality of the mind of the producer." Yet Flaubert had called for the author to efface himself. The resolution of this paradox for several writers around the turn of the century, including Joseph Conrad (1857–1924), Ford Madox Ford (1873–1939), and James himself, was either to interpose a fictional narrating intelligence between reader and author (like Lambert Strether in James's *The Ambassadors* [1903] or Charlie Marlow in Conrad's *Heart of Darkness* [1902]) or to narrate omnisciently but in an indirect, poetic, or ironic mode. Although literary impressionism was never a school like French naturalism — only Ford actually announced himself as being an impressionist — it was clearly a set of ideas about fiction that appealed not only to Ford and Conrad but also in some degree to Henry James, James Joyce, Virginia Woolf (1882–1941), Dorothy Richardson (1872–1957), Stephen Crane, and William Faulkner (1897–1962).

Impressionism took inspiration from the ideas of the impressionist painters, such as Claude Monet (1840–1926) and Edgar Degas (1834–1917), who were interested not in some external notion of objective reality but in the actual physical appearance of a scene to a perceiving eye. In his preface to *The Nigger of the "Narcissus"* (1897) Conrad defines his task as "by the power of the written word to make you hear, to make you feel — it is, before all, to make you see." This stress on immediate physical sensation rather than explanatory summary paralleled Monet's notoriously indistinct outlines, which aroused the wrath of the Parisian public. "Poor blind idiots," Monet commented. "They want to see everything clearly, even through the fog."[2] In impressionist writing, external, conventional description is often sacrificed for the immediacy of confusing perceptions — but also for an evocative vagueness that is conducive to the use of symbolism. As Conrad points out in the preface, "A work of art is very seldom limited to one exclusive meaning and not necessarily tending to a definite conclusion." In her essay "Modern Fiction" (1919) Virginia Woolf affirms that "life is not a series of gig lamps symmetrically arranged; but a luminous halo, a semi-transparent envelope surrounding us from the beginning of consciousness to the end." It is the modern novelist's task to "record the atoms as they fall upon the mind," however foggy or apparently chaotic the result may be.

In fact, impressionist writers tended to alternate between the claim that their sort of writing was a "realer" realism that abandoned simplistic nineteenth-century notions of objectivity and the claim that it was valuable because, to use Ford Madox Ford's favorite term, it registered the artist's unique "temperament." Certainly these writers put a premium on evoking the interiority of a character, whether through Marlow's extended metaphysical monologues, through the "stream of consciousness" of many of Woolf's protagonists, or through the endless self-examinations of James's narrators. With the rise of impressionism, the novel took a giant step inward, and there the "serious novel" was to remain for much of the twentieth century.

THE TWENTIETH CENTURY

Virtually all the commentary on the novel mentioned so far has come from professional novelists. During both the late eighteenth and the nineteenth centuries there was, of course, much discussion of novels in the circulating magazines, by reviewers and general essayists. But surprisingly little of this material has proved valuable. In the first place, for much of this period the novel was not generally considered to be a serious form of art worthy of serious consideration. Reviews were usually either simple plot summaries, strong expressions of approbation or derision (for reasons ranging from the idealistic to the commercial), or informal "appreciations" of well-bred literary dilettantes — these last usually of a kind that gave impressionism a bad name. The "man of letters" was an avocation in both Britain and America, and commercially at least it was a profession, but intellectually, it had little of the professional about it. With the rise of the study of English literature in British and American universities in the 1880s this situation began to change.

The professionalization of English literary studies had a variety of consequences for study of the novel and, eventually, for the novel itself. For example, by the late 1960s John Barth (b. 1930) was widely regarded as one of the most important American novelists writing, while he also taught in the Writing Workshops at Johns Hopkins University and published influential critical discussions of postmodernism in the novel. Given that Barth often wrote what was termed "metafiction" — fiction that was in some important way *about* fiction — it is obvious that in his career the separate figures of novelist, teacher, and critic had become inseparably entangled. And Barth was only the best known of a surprising number of postmodern author/critics in the academy after 1970.

But there were more immediate effects in the early twentieth century as the new profession sought to establish a working vocabulary and a field of study, or *canon*. It has been argued that literature (including the novel) was first taught as an "improving" and "ennobling" subject (rather than, say, as a mode of social criticism) because this was the most effective way for the new discipline to gain the support of the elites who determined the curriculum of higher education. Indeed, the Marxist critic Terry Eagleton has argued that literary studies in England were founded with the implied rationale that English literature helped define and promote essential Englishness and thus was a politically conservative institution.[3] If these analyses are accurate, the ruling elites must have been in for a rude awakening as literary study quickly began to assume and endorse the oppositional stance of virtually all significant modern writers.

Early Modern Novelists

In the first two decades of the century, though, the most interesting discussions of the novel were written by British novelists themselves, not by the dons of Oxford and Cambridge or the professors of Harvard and Yale. Oddly, after Henry James, prominent American novelists such as Ernest Hemingway, William Faulkner, and F. Scott Fitzgerald (1896–1940) had relatively little to say about the form. Perhaps the British modernists were more conscious of their membership in an avowedly revolutionary cultural movement and realized that the old rules no longer applied. In Virginia Woolf's essay "Modern Fiction," which discusses James Joyce specifically but applies perhaps better to her own work, she argues that "if a writer were a free man and not a slave" to the conventions of the literary marketplace, there would be in his novels "no plot, no comedy, no tragedy, no love interest, or catastrophe in the accepted style, and perhaps not a single button sewn on as the Bond Street tailors would have it." Woolf affirms in "Mr. Bennett and Mrs. Brown" that "all novels . . . deal with character," but insists that "the very widest interpretation can be put upon those words." D. H. Lawrence (1885–1930) is more radical: "You mustn't look in my novel for the old stable *ego* of character," he writes to Edward Garnett (1868–1937). "There is another *ego*, according to whose action the individual is unrecognizable, and passes through, as it were, allotropic states which it needs a deeper sense . . . to discover are states of the same radically unchanged element."

Even novelistic devices as apparently self-evident as conversation were suddenly in question. Ford Madox Ford writes of his collaboration with Conrad that they made it a rule "that no speech of one character could ever answer the speech that goes before it," because in life few people actually listen, being busy preparing their own speech. Perhaps the most important contribution to the theory of fiction was made by James Joyce in his concept of the "epiphany," a collection of which was compiled by his protagonist Stephen Dedalus. "By an epiphany he [Dedalus] meant a sudden spiritual manifestation, whether in the vulgarity of speech or of gesture or in a memorable phrase of the mind itself," Joyce explains in *Stephen Hero* (the early draft version of *A Portrait of the Artist as a Young Man*). Even ordinary bits of furniture, such as clocks, are capable of unexpected epiphanies, which may be recorded by the artist.[4] The epiphany has since become an accepted term for a fictional moment of realization, generally near the climax of a story, but in Stephen's usage it is a rather more mysterious moment in which something "spiritual" is shown by way of something material or even vulgar, such as daily speech recorded with all its hesitations, vagueness, and redundancy. Although Joyce might record ordinary speech in the same precise, reportorial way the naturalists did, he would have a very different aesthetic motive.

Perhaps the last important treatise on the novel by a major British novelist is E. M. Forster's (1879–1970) *Aspects of the Novel* (1927). A general discussion of how novels work, this book is divided almost chapter by chapter into "traditional" and "modernist" approaches: the chapters on story, character, and plot are fairly traditional, while in the chapters on "fantasy," "pattern and rhythm," and "prophecy" Forster tries to approach more volatile, poetic aspects of the novel in less familiar ways. To begin with, he makes his famous distinction between "flat" characters and "round" ones (see *character* in the glossary, p. 105) but also makes it clear that he shares Woolf's concept of character as something in perpetual flux, illuminated differently by different moments of experience.

Forster might be called a reluctant traditionalist: he admits with a sort of sigh that "oh dear, yes — the novel tells a story," but wishes that its most fundamental aspect "could be something different — melody, or perception of the truth, not this low atavistic form."[5] In the tradition of Flaubert and James, Forster is clearly more interested in the exploration of character in a novel than in mere incident. Indeed, Forster suggests that what he sees as the crowning achievement of the novel, pattern — which is closely related to rhythm, a term he uses somewhat like the repetitive leitmotif in a work of music — springs from plot but is not really dependent on it. There is nothing new about concern for what Fielding

later characterizes as "cultural materialism." Reading texts with the same sort of intensity and sensitivity the Leavises showed, Williams adds a perspective in which literary artifacts are also acknowledged to be the products of particular historical periods and social classes. Where Leavis idealizes his culture's "timeless classics" of the "great tradition," in *The English Novel from Dickens to Lawrence* (1970) Williams sees them as material for cultural consumption and judges them as politically progressive or reactionary — though never in any simplistic way. Where Leavis's (and the New Criticism's) point of departure is the transcendent value of the literary artist's "creative mind," Williams begins *The Long Revolution* with a political and social analysis of that very term, ending with a plea that art not be seen as a "separate order" but as a means of social communication — one means among others.[7]

The single most influential academic work on the origins of the novel in the Anglo-American tradition cannot be easily traced to either the Leavisite or the New Critical traditions, and though it has some affinities with the work of Williams it is far less inflected by Marxism. This is Ian Watt's *The Rise of the Novel: Studies in Defoe, Richardson, and Fielding* (1957). Watt was a fellow at Cambridge and acknowledged himself indebted to Q. D. Leavis's *Fiction and the Reading Public* (1932). But the analysis of the novel's beginnings that he offers has none of the evangelical quality of the Leavises' writings about culture. Where both Leavis and the New Critics established novelistic traditions in terms of the individual greatness of authors — their exceptionality — Watt's tradition relies upon what he sees as representative figures. Both the authors he discusses and their protagonists are portrayed by Watt as men and women of their class, time, and social milieu.

Watt sees as the basic characteristic of the novel its use of "formal realism." By this term he means to point to a group of "narrative procedures" that includes (1) the abandoning of traditional plots and "purple patches" of rhetoric and (2) the stress on developing individual characters and situations so that time, place, person, and even causation are given a new particularity. Alongside this argument about form, Watt develops the idea that the rise of the novel is bound up intimately with the rise of the middle class and middle-class individualism, with all the accompaniments of that social movement: the growth of capitalism, the spread of Protestantism, the growing influence of the commercial and industrial segments of society, and the increase in the reading public.[8] Philosophically, Watt also points to analogies between the formal realism of the novel and the philosophical realism of René Descartes (1596–1650) and John Locke (1632–1704). Both the method of Descartes and Locke and the logic of

the novel work from the collection of individual sense impressions out-
ward toward the mental construction of a universe.

Equally influential on readings of the novel was Wayne Booth's *The
Rhetoric of Fiction* (1961). Booth's book is unlike Watt's in that rather
than trying to establish an "origin" for the novel within the social and
intellectual currents of the eighteenth century, and so to arrive at a description of the "basic nature" of the novel, Booth specifically offers a
"rhetoric" of fiction. In his terms, this is a study not of what a work *is*, but
of what it *does*, or "the kinds of actions authors perform on readers."[9]
Booth's approach, called "neo-Aristotelian" because it descends from
Aristotle's *Poetics* and *Rhetoric*, differs substantially from that of the New
Critics, especially because he gives the Jamesian novel no preference over
novels with a narrator as intrusive as those of Thackeray or Fielding. Rather
than a self-enclosed verbal artifact, Booth sees the novel as an imitation
of the real world, in the rich sense in which Aristotle uses the term *imitation*. Rather than viewing the author as the indirect promoter of some
aesthetic contemplativeness, he sees authors as wishing to move readers
in specific ways, often by teaching them truths about the world. Because
he is interested in readers' reactions to what they are told and to the way
it is told, Booth frequently discusses "reliable" and "unreliable" narrators.
Another term of Booth's that has come into wide usage is the "implied
author," for the suggested, idealized versions of themselves (and their
values) that authors create through their novels.

By appearing to privilege the domestic, Richardsonian novel of psychological density, Watt can be seen as having overly restricted the novel
by "defining" it through a single strain. The major challenge to Watt's
formulations has come in Michael McKeon's *The Origins of the English
Novel, 1600–1740* (1987), which also usefully analyzes other major critical works on the novel. McKeon points out that while Watt's argument
works very well for the middle-class Richardson and Defoe and their novels, it works less well for the aristocratic Fielding, whose novels are still
enmeshed in the romance tradition. Like Watt McKeon points out that
Erich Auerbach's influential *Mimesis: The Representation of Reality in
Western Literature* (1946; trans., 1953) foregrounds formal realism in the
novel's development. By implication, it devalues the elements of romance,
fantasy, and verbal play that continue to haunt the novel even in the heyday of formal realism and become prominent in the twentieth century.
Indeed, Auerbach's appreciation of the narrative innovations of major
modernists such as Joyce and Woolf is very limited.

McKeon discusses a wide variety of prose fictions that lead into the
novel, such as saints' lives and exploration narratives, and has a substan-

tial chapter on Cervantes' *Don Quixote*, surely a glaring omission from Watt's book. Finally, from a theoretical standpoint, McKeon sets against Watt's defining of the novel as a historical and social product Northrop Frye's "archetypal" approach to literature: in *The Anatomy of Criticism* (1957) Frye derives all literary forms ultimately from myth, thus rendering them timeless and ahistorical. Frye sees five primary "modes" that displace one another in history — the mythical, romantic, high mimetic, low mimetic, and ironic — and in so doing implies that the basic matter of the classical and modern novel (which employ the low mimetic and ironic forms) is merely a transformation of the timeless seasonal truths carried by myth and romance. Frye's vision of literature has often been called overly literary, formalist, and unhistorical; but perhaps by that token Watt's vision of the novel is not literary enough.

The Rise of Theory

Despite their numerous differences, all the perspectives on the novel discussed so far might fairly be seen within the Western humanist tradition. But starting in the 1960s a series of intellectual movements from Europe became influential in America (and, more gradually, in England as well) that could not easily be characterized as humanist. One well-known essay symbolizing this shift is Roland Barthes's (1915–1980) "The Death of the Author" (1968), in which he announces, "We know now that a text consists not of a line of words, releasing a single 'theological' meaning (the 'message' of the Author-God), but of a multi-dimensional space in which are married and contested several writings, none of which is original."[10] Barthes is somewhat unclear as to whether he is discussing a literary movement beginning with the poet Stéphane Mallarmé (1842–1898) in which authors consciously "distance themselves," a philosophical shift in the way modern writing is seen by critics, or even a change in the entire notion of authorship that comes with our contemporary condition. Whichever of these alternatives is in force, it is sure that the interest of the advanced critic has shifted (in the title of another Barthes essay) "From Work to Text" — from the idea of a unified literary work whose importance and integrity is underwritten by the authority of its author to anonymous text. The "text" in this sense is without claims to unity or integrity, is produced by complex cultural currents, and to a great extent is enabled by the newly active reader.

Barthes usually addresses writing in general, opposing an old-fashioned, "classic," "readerly" writing practice (or critical perception — the distinction is not always clear) to one that is avant-garde, "modern," or "writerly."

He is an enthusiast of Alain Robbe-Grillet's "new novel," an experimental sort of novel that Robbe-Grillet (b. 1922) describes and defends in his polemic *For a New Novel* (1963; trans., 1965). What Robbe-Grillet and Barthes champion is a kind of text that subverts the conventional processes of gathering meaning that a reader employs with ordinary novels. "New novels" particularly do violence to the idea of a narrator, since frequently no remotely human point of view can easily be posited as the source of the minutely detailed objective descriptions of a novel like Robbe-Grillet's *Jealousy* (1957; trans., 1959). Such texts were often called "anti-novels" for this reason — although it is undeniable that such subversions of the effects of mimetic fiction are themselves dependent on the conventions they mock. Eventually these anti-novels were classed with a growing body of literature described as "postmodern" and discussion of them was increasingly carried on under that title (see chap. 3).

By the 1970s, under the influence of the structuralist or semiotic approach championed by Barthes and others, the balance of critical interest was shifting from "novel" to "narration," from questions of mimesis and (in Booth's wake) the ethical situation of the implied author to questions about the text's linguistic effects and the narrative system that constituted it. The emphasis was on structural analysis, ways of describing what happens in narration without necessary reference to the author. The most famous such analysis was *S/Z* (1970; trans., 1976), in which Barthes discusses a novella by Balzac in terms of five "codes," frequently on a sentence-by-sentence basis. The codes are the *proairetic*, a code of actions, which dictates the reader's construction of plot; the *hermeneutic*, referring to questions and answers, mysteries and solutions within the plot; the *semic*, which involves semantic features the reader uses to develop characters and identify persons; the *symbolic*, which guides the reader's extrapolations toward thematic and symbolic readings; and the *referential*, which points toward an accepted, stereotyped body of cultural knowledge assumed by the text. Although Barthes calls his semiotics a "science" and claims to have derived it from the theoretical linguistics of Ferdinand de Saussure and Émile Benveniste, most commentators have found these codes rather arbitrary. Jonathan Culler, for one, has suggested that a code referring to the process of narration itself should have been included in Barthes's list — although it is possible that acknowledging such a code might drag in the implication of human agency that Barthes is otherwise so careful to avoid.[11]

In widening their critical target to include not just the novel but all storytelling, structuralists founded the approach known as "narratology." This was based originally on the work of the Russian formalists, a group of linguistic thinkers most active in Moscow between 1915 and 1926. The formalists most frequently mentioned by critics of the 1960s and 1970s were Roman Jakobson, Viktor Shklovski, and Boris Eikhenbaum. A key formalist concept was Shklovski's "defamiliarization," denoting the unusual linguistic or literary practices that can make familiar things appear strange; defamiliarization, it was felt, especially characterized modern texts. But most structuralist analyses of narrative took as their point of departure Vladimir Propp's *Morphology of the Folktale* (1928). Propp feels that by ignoring the identity of characters, folktales can be reduced to thirty-one basic "functions," which are something like "actions with significance for the course of the plot"; different tales might vary the characters involved, but if the sequence of "functions" is the same, then the tales are essentially identical, even if certain functions are omitted.

Elaborating Propp's ideas, A. G. Greimas evolved a theory in which narratives are analyzed in terms of six "actants" (such as "subject looking for the object"). In a group of seminal books in the late 1960s and early 1970s, Gérard Genette laid the foundations of the modern study of narrative discourse (see *point of view* in the glossary, p. 118). Following him, narratologists such as Seymour Chatman, Gerald Prince, Dorrit Cohn, and Shlomith Rimmon-Kenan have greatly elaborated the study, treating "discourse," or the actual presentation of events, with the same attention as "story," the abstractable sequence of events themselves. They have cast light not only on narrative structure but on the possible "speeds" and conciseness with which narratives can convey actions; on the types of "focalization" (or presentation through an implied consciousness) and detailing of events it can feature; and on the basic means narration offers of depicting thoughts and utterances. All these were perfectly acceptable areas of investigation within the humanist Anglo-American tradition, but it took the European intervention of the 1960s to invigorate the enterprise.

Marxist Accents

Although contemporary views of the novel are heavily influenced by the work of the structuralists and their immediate heirs, it is arguable that they are equally shaped by Marxist approaches. Karl Marx (1818–1883) himself praised novelists such as Dickens, Thackeray, and Charlotte Brontë, asserting that they revealed more political and social truths than all the politicians and moralists of the world (see chap. 2 for a brief account of Marx's thought). During the twentieth century, however, some of Marx's followers, especially under the influence of Stalinism, took the position that any art that did not directly advocate the overthrow of the ruling class and the rise of the proletariat was bad art. Modernist art in particular was castigated for degenerate "subjectivism" and "psychologism," an inappropriate and counterrevolutionary concern for the interior life of the bourgeois subject. Further, the difficulty of modernist texts was seen by orthodox communists as an insult to or an effort to exclude the working class. But the Marxist thinkers who have been influential in the Anglo-American discussion have been primarily the "Western Marxists," who opposed the official Stalinist line on literature and generally tried to reconcile Marx's goals and analytical tools with their own commitments to democracy and humanist values.

Among these, Gyorgy Lukács (1885–1971) is best known for his defense of nineteenth-century realism. His pre-Marxist *Theory of the Novel* (1916; trans., 1971), indebted to the philosopher Georg Hegel (1770–1831), portrays the novel as an appropriate genre for an age of transition in which values are lost and the individual is alienated. In *The Historical Novel* (1937; trans., 1962) Lukács calls historical authenticity the basis of aesthetic evaluation. But despite that unpromising premise he has sensitive essays on nineteenth-century novelists, especially Sir Walter Scott, showing how their works portray subtle and overt class conflicts and social oppression within a concrete historical context. Lukács, like Auerbach, is unsympathetic to what he considers "decadent" modernist art — a position in which he is opposed by other Western Marxists, especially Bertolt Brecht, Ernst Bloch, and Theodor Adorno. Adorno, for example, takes the view that twentieth-century writers who still use the form of the standard realist novel are making a reactionary political statement because they do not reflect the chaos of contemporary life the way the work of James Joyce does.

The Marxist thinker with the greatest impact outside Marxist circles over the past two decades has been Mikhail Bakhtin (1895–1975), a Russian influenced by the formalists who spent much of his life in "internal exile" and obscurity and was rediscovered only near the end of his life, in the early 1960s. His impact in America may in part be due to the fact that it is unclear just how Marxist he is. Two important undoubtedly Marxist works often attributed to Bakhtin were in fact published under the names of associates of his, while the three major books (all in English translation) that are undoubtedly his are not necessarily incompatible with some sort of neo-Marxism, but are not obviously indebted to Marx's thought either. Bakhtin has been construed as a formalist, a Marxist, an anti-Marxist, a humanist pluralist, a proto-poststructuralist, and a radical Russian Orthodox Christian; but in fact, he evades any simple label.

Bakhtin began in the early 1920s as a neo-Kantian philosopher concerned with ethics and aesthetics but soon turned to a concentration on the word. This culminated in his *Problems of Dostoevski's Poetics* (1929; rev. ed., trans., 1984), which explores what Bakhtin calls the "dialogic" potential of language in the novel. Language is dialogical when it is generated by at least two embodied voices or persons: when we speak, we are generally speaking *toward* at least one other person, in anticipation or response, and our voice itself is formed of a multitude of other voices. This is the condition of living language; dead language is "monologism," a voice (like that of the Church in the medieval period) that admits of no other voice's existence. For Bakhtin, poetry is usually monologic and thus inferior to the novel, which is potentially the most dialogical, and thus the highest, art form. Bakhtin delights in anatomizing the ways in which language in a novel can be "double-voiced," or reflect more than one linguistic center.

A second major concept for Bakhtin is "carnival," developed in *Rabelais and His World* (1968), a book originally written as a doctoral dissertation in 1940. In the folk ritual of carnival, in which for a brief period of licensed anarchy all traditional values are inverted and the "lower stratum" of a communal, immortal body is celebrated, Bakhtin locates a model for the urge toward liberating transgression that is deep in folk consciousness and can be found in writers like François Rabelais (c. 1483–1553).

Because of his preference for the liberating laughter of carnival and the "polyphonic" quality of novels in which the author's voice has no privilege over the fully realized voices of characters, Bakhtin suggests an alternative tradition of the novel. In several of the essays collected in *The Dialogic Imagination: Four Essays* (1981) Bakhtin suggests that he would endorse the formalist Shklovski's paradox that Laurence Sterne's (1713–1768) *Tristram Shandy* (1759–1767) is "the most typical novel in world literature."[12] For Bakhtin, there is a line from third-century B.C. Menippean satires and dialogues through *Don Quixote*, Rabelais, Defoe's *Moll Flanders*, Fielding's *Tom Jones*, Aleksandr Pushkin (1799–1837), *Tristram Shandy*, some of Tobias Smollett (1721–1771) and Dickens, on up to the novels of Fyodor Dostoevsky (1821–1881) and (many would argue, though perhaps for political reasons Bakhtin does not list it) Joyce's *Ulysses*. Bakhtin in fact portrays the novel as a "super genre," one that can assimilate the other genres at will and that, in its essentially dialogical function, can be bound by no other formal principles.

Poststructuralist Criticism

Insofar as they have a political thrust, all of the foregoing approaches to the novel share what can be called the "subversive hypothesis": they presume that novels, and indeed all forms of literature, are innately on the side of individual freedom, or at least in some way affirm a constellation of humane values. Such an assumption has been built into the rationale of literary study from its institutional beginnings in the nineteenth century, despite the fact that the New Criticism, like some modernist writers, officially took the position that literature is above or apart from particular moral assertions. But the rise of poststructuralist criticism in the 1970s and 1980s has challenged that kind of assumption, and indeed the core assumptions of humanism generally. For thinkers such as Jacques Derrida (b. 1930), Jacques Lacan (1901–1981), the later Roland Barthes, and Michel Foucault (1926–1984), works of literature participate in "discourse," a system of signification that always exceeds any intended "message" and always escapes any individual "center" or controlling "self." This realization, as Derrida first asserted, cuts against the grain of Western metaphysics since Plato.

Criticism in the line of Derrida, often called "deconstruction," has seldom produced "readings" of novels in a conventional sense, though it often uses the text of novels as a point of departure. Some deconstructive critics rely heavily on philosophical play with words suggested by the text they are examining; for them, the question of whether the philosophical issue is "supported by" the text, much less the author, is irrelevant, since any text turns attention toward the free play of language. A more structured form of deconstruction can be represented by J. Hillis Miller's *Fiction and Repetition: Seven English Novels* (1982). In Hardy's novels, for example, Miller finds a "personification, concretely presented in the lives and minds of the characters, of the basic metaphysical beliefs which have been instinctive to mankind for millennia: belief in origin, end, and underlying ground making similarities identities, belief in the literal truth of the trope of personification."[13] But meanwhile, the "other side" of the novel, at the level of its language, images, and metaphors, undoes these identifications and displays a series of gaps, absences, silences, and disruptive differences that destroy the illusion of metaphysical unity. Unusual among deconstructive critics, Miller continues to practice a kind of "close reading" such as the New Critics depend on, but it might be called close reading with a minus sign.

Aside from Derrida the other most influential poststructuralist thinker, Michel Foucault, has stressed somewhat interchangeable ideas of discourse and power, in which each is a pervasive system that is controlled by no one and no group but exercises some control over everyone it touches. For Foucault, Western civilization since the eighteenth-century Enlightenment is marked by increasing control over the lives and thoughts of citizens, a control particularly manifested by the generation of a discourse that constructs and defines identity, sickness and health, normality and abnormality — and thus linguistically pervades every aspect of human life. For Foucault and for "New Historicist" and neo-Marxist literary critics who have followed him, there is no essential difference between novels and other documents; because "reality" is always arbitrarily constructed by texts, psychology textbooks and novels are equally fictive. The novel is no longer seen as a passive reflector of society, or even as a distorting mirror. For these critics, the same forces that participate in determining identity and gender roles in society do so in fiction; and furthermore, novels themselves are part of the overall discourse that helps determine these things. A notable example of "negative" Foucauldian criticism of the novel is D. A. Miller's *The Novel and the Police* (1988), in which Miller examines the novel's disciplinary role as a contributor to the discourse of social regimentation.[14] It may clarify both theories to consider that this approach is the polar opposite of that of Bakhtin, who sees the novel's voice as a liberating polyphony.

NOTES

1. This is an argument first fully elaborated in Richard Chase, *The American Novel and Its Tradition* (New York: Doubleday, 1957).

2. Quoted in Watt, *Conrad in the Nineteenth Century* (Berkeley: U of California P, 1979) 170. From Jean Renoir, *Renoir My Father.*

3. Terry Eagleton, *Literary Theory: An Introduction* (Minneapolis: U of Minnesota P, 1983) 28.

4. From James Joyce, *Stephen Hero,* ed. Theodore Spencer (New York: New Directions, 1959) 211.

5. E. M. Forster, *Aspects of the Novel* (New York: Harcourt, 1956 [1927]) 45.

6. Dorothy Van Ghent, *The English Novel: Form and Function* (New York: Harper, 1953) 3, 6, 7.

7. Raymond Williams, *The Long Revolution,* rev. ed. (New York: Harper, 1966) 39.

8. Although Watt's presumption that the middle class "rose" during the eighteenth century is a staple of Anglo-American criticism, it is not at all obvious that this is the case, or how one should define "rose." Franco Moretti, for instance, argues that the middle class did not actually rise until the vast bureaucratization of the twentieth century. See Moretti, *The Way of the World: The* Bildungsroman *in European Culture* (London: Verso, 1987) 230n5.

9. Wayne Booth, "*The Rhetoric of Fiction* and the Poetics of Fiction," *Novel* 1 (1968): 115.

10. Roland Barthes, "The Death of the Author," *The Rustle of Language,* trans. Richard Howard (New York: Hill and Wang, 1986) 52–53.

11. Jonathan Culler, *Structuralist Poetics: Structuralism, Linguistics, and the Study of Literature* (Ithaca: Cornell UP, 1975) 203.

12. Viktor Shklovski, "Sterne's *Tristram Shandy*: Stylistic Commentary," *Russian Formalist Criticism: Four Essays,* ed. Lee T. Lemon and Marion J. Reis (Lincoln: U of Nebraska P, 1965) 57.

13. J. Hillis Miller, *Fiction and Repetition: Seven English Novels* (Cambridge: Harvard UP, 1982) 15.

14. D. A. Miller, *The Novel and the Police* (Berkeley: U of California P, 1988).

2

The Rise of Modernism

When we set off a given period for special study — the twentieth century, say, or the "modern" period, which may not be the same thing — we are performing an admittedly arbitrary act. There are good reasons why we do so, reasons both institutional, having to do with how literature is taught in the academy, and intellectual, having to do with the necessity of drawing boundaries before we can discuss anything. Late nineteenth-century writers and critics believed in the study of discrete historical periods, on the assumption that coherent cultural periods had a distinct Zeitgeist, or spirit of the times, and that that spirit could be detected in any smaller segment of time or group of artifacts chosen for study. This in turn depended upon a faith that objective knowledge of history was attainable, and it was often accompanied by the assumption that a certain cumulative progress was somehow embodied in "the march of history." The twentieth century has abandoned the belief in this traditional sort of "historicism," but without abandoning the need for literary history or the conviction that literature is importantly involved with history.

THE MODERN BREAK

If we were simply to choose the year 1900 as a dividing line, we would discover some interesting items that hint at a large change. In 1900 Max Planck first set forth the quantum theory that is fundamental to nuclear physics; in that year also, William Crookes separated out uranium. Gregor Mendel's work on heredity was rediscovered. Sigmund Freud's *Interpretation of Dreams* was published (an event symbolic of the widening importance of symbolism itself). The critic John Ruskin died aged and honored, and Oscar Wilde died prematurely, disgraced and in exile. Stephen Crane died young and Friedrich Nietzsche died insane; both men would become far more identified with the century to come than with the century in which they had lived and written. The Labour Party — basically a party of protest against middle-class policies that was based on working-class support — was founded in England at the height of the Boer War. As for technology, the "modern world" was rapidly taking shape. In 1900 the first zeppelin flew and the first wireless speech was sent. The previous year had seen the invention of magnetic sound recording and the deployment of the first bus in London — and, as if in response to the headaches of modernity, the marketing of aspirin. In the following year, with exquisite timing, Queen Victoria died after a lifetime spanning nearly a century, ushering in the brief Edwardian age of her socialite son, a kind of Indian summer before the Great War broke out in 1914.

The turn of the century itself encouraged a sense of crisis and discontinuity, as ends of centuries generally do. Everywhere new movements were the rage — the New Spirit, New Paganism, New Realism, and New Drama in the arts, and the troubling figure of the New Woman sometimes glimpsed on the streets or on the stage. In his autobiographical *Education of Henry Adams* (1906) the American writer described attending the Great Exposition in Paris in 1900. Adams (1838–1918) felt "his historical neck broken by the irruption of forces totally new." The giant dynamos terrified him, and he felt them as a sort of moral force. In a short seven years, he felt, "man had translated himself into a new universe which had no common scale of measurement with the old." A child born in 1900 would be "born into a new world which would be not a unity but a multiple."

But while the general sense of change was mounting during the 1890s, the old century and its values were slow to die. In 1887 in Chickering Hall in New York there was a benefit reading for the American Copyright League to encourage the formation of international copyright laws; at this point British literature was still being printed in America copyright-free, and American authors correspondingly suffered. The reading featured the most notable American literary figures of the time, James Russell Lowell (1819–1891), Oliver Wendell Holmes (1809–1894), John Greenleaf Whittier (1807–1892), Mark Twain (1835–1910), Edward Eggleston (1837–1902), George Washington Cable (1844–1925), and James

Whitcomb Riley (1849–1916) among them. Lowell, Holmes, and Whittier represented the "genteel tradition" of letters; Cable and Twain were seen as regionalists and humorists; and Riley, perhaps the most popular of all, was the Hoosier songster who wrote homespun verse in a local dialect.

Walt Whitman, of course, was considered a wild man and beyond the pale, and Emily Dickinson was as yet unknown. Theodore Dreiser, whose publisher withdrew *Sister Carrie* in 1900, was far too young and too radical to be considered to speak. After all, his protagonist Carrie had chosen to live as the mistress of a wealthy man and had not been crushingly punished for doing so. Dreiser's fellow writer Ellen Glasgow (1873–1945), speaking for the new generation unrepresented on the platform, commented, "They were important and they knew it. . . . When they were not . . . 'encouraging one another in mediocrity,' they were gravely preparing work for one another to praise. For this reason, no doubt, they impressed me with a kind of evergreen optimism. They were elderly, but not yet mature."[1] It was with a similar mixture of respect and contempt that Virginia Woolf discussed the dominant British novelists of 1900, including H. G. Wells, Arnold Bennett, and John Galsworthy — of whom all but Wells are now mostly forgotten.

Perhaps it was not coincidence that two more than ordinarily shameful wars broke out around the turn of the century. In 1898 the United States embarked on the brief Spanish-American War, driving Spain from Cuba, where there were substantial American business interests. The war was encouraged by William Randolph Hearst and Joseph Pulitzer, two powerful newspaper publishers, and was pursued despite Spanish efforts to capitulate. It marked the end of the old Spanish empire in the New World and an important step toward the new sort of imperialism that would characterize much of the "American century."

In 1899 the Anglo-Boer War broke out in the Transvaal and the Orange Free State, two South African states settled by the Boers, farmers of Dutch descent. Spurred by Cecil John Rhodes, head of the British South Africa Company, the Crown attempted to form an economic union embracing the entirety of southern Africa and to challenge Boer authority. Although the war ended in a British victory in 1902, the Boers fought far more successfully than the British public had expected them to, and serious incompetence in the British staff was revealed. Ironically, the war led to a revival of ethnic consciousness among the Dutch-descended Afrikaners, and the beginning of the end for Great Britain's worldwide empire; rebellions in China, India, and numerous other colonized areas erupted yearly, and the liberal press was beginning to report some of the worst colonial abuses. Joseph Conrad's exposé of Belgium's barbarism in the Congo, *Heart of Darkness* (1902), was only the best-known example of the genre. If we can see the nineteenth century as preoccupied with the old and the new worlds — the European powers and America, and their relationship — then the twentieth is increasingly concerned with Europe and America's relationship with the third world.

Meanwhile, a massive series of social changes was establishing the world we call modern. Industrialization had accelerated throughout the nineteenth century, until by far the largest part of both the "laboring classes" and the middle class was engaged in nonagricultural manufacturing and production or in the service industries that followed rapidly upon urbanization. At the same time, a majority of families were only one or two generations removed from the land, a situation that produced a shared myth of the rural past among city dwellers. Major cities expanded into metropolises and smaller cities grew at the expense of the countryside. By the turn of the century 78 percent of the inhabitants of Great Britain lived in cities and towns.[2] The word *suburbia* was coined in the 1890s, already carrying a pejorative connotation.

The quality of life within the cities was changing as a result of industry as well. Around the turn of the century modern mass transit systems, including electrified trams, were being installed in large cities. Along with the use of alarm clocks and the rationalization of working hours, the new century saw the development of rush hour, traffic jams, and other effects of the industrial regimentation of humanity. The means of mass communication were developing, including the telegraph and, increasingly with the new century, the telephone. At the same time, methods of communication that would come to be known as the "mass media" — newly influential newspapers, followed in the next decades by the cinema and radio — were beginning to take on portentous outlines. Enthusiasts of technology, such as the Italian futurist Filippo Marinetti, argued that a "complete renewal of human sensibility" was being brought about by these products of technology, because "means of communication, transportation and information have a decisive effect on the psyche."[3]

In the late nineteenth century, inexpensive magazines and book editions became economically feasible, while the late-nineteenth-century Education Acts in England were bearing fruit in a new readership. Probably both the "high" art for an aesthetic minority — what came to be known as modernism — and the "popular" or "mass" art that modernism seemed to reject were made possible by the spread of literacy beyond the leisured classes. While the entertainment industries were forming genres tailored to particular tastes within the mass market (like the detective story and the popular romance), British subjects and American citizens could reasonably feel that they were gaining individuality through the new commodities being offered to them and that they were simultaneously being defined as part of a mass market. The bicycle and the private automobile, both of which were disseminated rapidly after 1900, allowed individuals far greater freedom of movement than they had had before, but at the price of a new regimentation of traffic.

Insofar as there was a bourgeois public consciousness at the turn of the century, it was dedicated to rational enlightenment, the conviction that, with the help of reason, civilization had improved and was daily improving further the lot of everyone. The prestige of the sciences had never been higher; the nineteenth-century explosion of technology had demonstrated that science not only progressed in its own terms but had rapid and enormous effects on people's lives. Medicine was finally emerging from its protracted dark ages, and procedures such as asepsis and anesthesia (Queen Victoria was the first well-known patient to deliver a baby under ether) were successfully established. In some ways, a belief in rational progress had actually displaced religious belief.

The social sciences or human sciences were developing, with thinkers like John Dewey and Max Weber attempting to lay down bases for the study of human societies. Indeed, it was Weber who suggested that the form of thinking that had become dominant by the turn of the century was "instrumental reason," a form he criticized as being divorced from any inherently reasonable ends. One illustration of the dominance of instrumental rationality was the work of Francis Galton and Karl Pearson, who attempted to found the science of eugenics, perhaps the most direct attempt to apply the methods of positivistic science to the study and controlled breeding of human beings. Although Galton's and Pearson's dreams were not implemented, both England and the United States were increasingly run by a new managerial class eager to implement principles of rational efficiency. There was a rage for the American Frederick Taylor's time and motion studies, set forth in his *Principles of Scientific Management* (1911).

What sort of change, if any, did the new century herald? With her tongue partly in her cheek, Virginia Woolf claimed that "on or about December, 1910, human character changed,"[4] thus giving voice to the modernist conviction that modern man (and modern woman) was in some way essentially different from humanity (or just British humanity?) under Victoria's reign. She may have chosen 1910 in honor of her friend Roger Fry's exhibition of postimpressionist art in London; but Randall Stevenson has pointed out that that date had important political implications as well: "following the General Election in that month . . . it became clear that the

Liberal Government could, if necessary, abolish the powers of the House of Lords if forced to do so in order to carry out its program of radical reform."[5] As it happens, 1910 was the year in which William Faulkner's character Quentin Compson in *The Sound and the Fury* (1929) commits suicide, thus bringing to an end a supposedly noble southern lineage (though Woolf, of course, could not have appreciated this). The cumulative effect of all these changes of emphasis, evolutions in the material conditions in living, and altered perceptions is the condition known as modernity — a very different thing, of course, from modernism, an aesthetic movement representing in part a willed rebellion against the modern condition.

But particularly among recent critics and philosophers it has been argued that the twentieth century involved an even more sweeping change in the overall *episteme* (Foucault's term), the grounds of knowledge. Jacques Derrida has argued that there is a "rupture," a "moment" around the turn of the century in which "language invaded the universal problematic," and "everything became discourse." The implications of such claims are not obvious, but Derrida wants to point to a removal of either the divine or the human presence as authority or justification for systems of knowledge, for the first time in history. Derrida traces this change to Friedrich Nietzsche's critique of metaphysics, Sigmund Freud's critique of the classical concept of the self, and Martin Heidegger's "destruction of metaphysics," all of which indicate a period from roughly 1880 to 1930.[6] When Derrida speaks of language he means to allude to Ferdinand de Saussure's vision of language as an autonomous system, theorized in his *Course in General Linguistics* (1916) and adapted by many contemporary thinkers as a model for other human systems. But in fact there was a general recognition in the early years of the century that language provides a shaky foundation for all kinds of knowledge. The protagonist of Dorothy Richardson's (1873–1957) novel series *Pilgrimage* (1915–1967) complains, "*All* that has been said and known in the world is in *language*, in words. . . . The meaning of words change with people's thought. Then no one *knows* anything for certain. Everything depends upon the way a thing is put, and that is a question of some particular civilization."[7]

There is no question that several sorts of relativism were "in the air" after the turn of the century, but for critics who are more inclined to look to concrete historical events as a cause of any cultural break, the obvious candidate is World War I. Although we usually date modernism as a movement between 1890 and 1940, the major modernist achievements tend to cluster in the 1920s, the decade immediately following the war. For instance, in the *annus mirabilis* of 1922 Joyce's *Ulysses* was published, along with T. S. Eliot's (1888–1965) *The Waste Land*; Sinclair Lewis's (1885–1951) *Babbitt*, a condemnation of middle-class, small-town America; Katherine Mansfield's (1888–1923) *The Garden Party*; and Virginia Woolf's *Jacob's Room*, a novel about a young man whose life is abruptly ended by the war and which itself ends just as abruptly. In 1922 also, T. S. Eliot was given the editorship of an important new literary journal, the *Criterion*, thus giving modern writing an institutional voice.

It has often been argued that the Great War caused an unprecedented revolution in the general outlook in England and the European countries because of the unprecedented slaughter, the unprecedented involvement of "noncombatants," and the unprecedented scale of the demonstration of bureaucratized, technologically assisted inhumanity. Paul Fussell pursues these themes in *The Great War and Modern Memory* (1975), arguing that the war was "more ironic than any before or since" because it was a public embarrassment to the idea of progress and meliorism. He quotes Henry James at the outbreak of war: "The plunge of civilization into this abyss of blood and darkness . . . is a thing that so gives away the whole long age during which we have supposed the world to be . . . gradually bettering, that to have to take it all now for what the treacherous years were all the while really making for and *meaning* is too tragic for any words."[8]

For participants in the war, the experience of trench warfare was generally enough to explode the inflated rhetoric of patriotism and sacrifice that had led to huge enlistments and public enthusiasm at the war's beginning. In 1914 Wilfred Owen (1893–1918) wrote:

> O meet it is and passing sweet
> To live in peace with others,
> But sweeter still and far more meet,
> To die in war for brothers.

By 1920, he was bitterly assuring his readers that if they had witnessed the death from poison gas of a soldier,

> . . . you would not tell with such high zest
> To children ardent for some desperate glory,
> The old Lie: Dulce et decorum est
> Pro patria mori.

And if it was no longer "sweet and meet to die for one's country," Hemingway's Lieutenant Frederic Henry in *A Farewell to Arms* (1929) had always found himself "embarrassed by the words sacred, glorious, and sacrifice." In the war he "had seen nothing sacred, and the things that were glorious had no glory and the sacrifices were like the stockyards at

Chicago." Abstract words like *glory, honor, courage,* and *hallow* he found "obscene."[9] Much of the obscenity came from the fact that such words were usually invoked by those at home who had no concept of the realities of modern warfare, and Henry's feelings here reflect a soldier's alienation from those for whom he is fighting — a revulsion that was all too widespread.

The argument of those who see the war as the decisive break, then, is that the massive disenchantment with sentimental patriotism generalized itself in a feeling of rejection of the older generation's entire set of values. It seemed to many that an art expressing a new sensibility and new values would have to reject conventional forms. Certainly there was a strong linkage between rejection of the war and aesthetic experimentation. James Joyce both by personal conviction and as an Irishman was a noncombatant. Many artists and intellectuals among Virginia Woolf's Bloomsbury group were pacifists, as was D. H. Lawrence, who had married Frieda von Richthofen, a cousin of the notorious German flying ace the Red Baron.

Among American writers the linkage was not so strong, partly because of America's belated entry into the war and different experience of it, but novels like *A Farewell to Arms* convey a similar disillusion, while E. E. Cummings's *The Enormous Room* (1922), which portrays the poet's imprisonment in a French detention camp for challenging authority, captures an atmosphere of existential absurdity long before existentialist philosophy came to public attention in the 1940s. But the problem with positing the war as the essential break in experience, at least from the point of view of literary history, is that some important novelists, such as James and Conrad, and poets, such as Ezra Pound (1885–1972) and Eliot, were already doing substantially modernist work before the war ever broke out. Indeed, the historian Eric J. Hobsbawm has noted,

> By 1914 virtually everything that can take shelter under the broad and rather undefined category "modernism" was already in place: cubism; expressionism; futurism; pure abstraction in painting; functionalism and flight from ornament in architecture; the abandonment of tonality in music; the break with tradition in literature.[10]

THE MODERNIST CANON

Just who were the modernist writers? The most common usage of the term *modernism* refers to the work of writers who formed a self-conscious avant-garde around the time of World War I. Writers most frequently named include T. S. Eliot and Ezra Pound (Americans writing in Britain); D. H. Lawrence and Virginia Woolf (both British); the Anglo-Irish poet W. B. Yeats (1865–1939); and James Joyce (an Irishman writing in Europe). Slightly later the Americans Ernest Hemingway; F. Scott Fitzgerald, a more conventional writer; Gertrude Stein (1874–1946), a much less conventional one; and especially William Faulkner came to be included in the roster. However, none of these figures are regarded as "true modernists" or "high modernists" (practicing the most extreme form of modernism) *throughout* their careers. In general the decade of the 1920s is seen as the high-water mark of modernism. Following the 1920s, most "serious" literary work has been seen as less radically experimental than the writing of that decade — or, in some cases, as headed in an appreciably different experimental direction that literary historians call "postmodernism."

We should note that a list of authors such as the one above is remarkable for its exclusions. Only one woman appears — and at least one prominent critic, Hugh Kenner, refuses to call Virginia Woolf a modernist at all. Others, however, have pointed out that women who played historically important roles and who produced very substantial writing, such as May Sinclair (1865–1946), the writer H.D. (Hilda Doolittle) (1886–1961), Dorothy Richardson, and Katherine Mansfield, for years were quietly "written out" of the canon (that is, the accepted academic list of writers to be studied).[11] We might also note that Wyndham Lewis (1882–1957), who was seen by both Eliot and Pound as one of the most important modernist writers, is seldom read or discussed, for complicated reasons involving politics and personality, and that African American writers, including those of the Harlem Renaissance of the 1920s, are also often excluded.

Finally, we should keep in mind that modernism was, if nothing else, an *international* aesthetic movement, involving artists and writers from a multitude of countries and frequently featuring writers who were somehow geographically displaced. Joyce, born and raised in Ireland, lived his entire adult life on the Continent, especially in Paris and in international cities like Trieste and Zurich; similarly, the latter part of Lawrence's life was one continuous exile from England. Such writers were especially susceptible to the influence of Continental writers and in turn influenced them: Joyce's *Ulysses* was more famous in Paris for many years than in London or New York. It is difficult to appreciate the shape of modernist writing without reading, for instance, Fyodor Dostoevsky, Anton Chekhov (1860–1904), Marcel Proust (1871–1922), Thomas Mann (1875–1955), André Gide (1869–1951), or Rainer Maria Rilke (1875–1926), although because of the organization of British and American universities, students often discover the English-speaking modernists in a misleading state of isolation.

INTELLECTUAL PRECURSORS

In 1965 Richard Ellmann and Charles Feidelson published a book paradoxically entitled *The Modern Tradition* that compiled literary and philosophical documents they thought important for understanding modernism. The readings included documents by early romantic poets, which gives some idea of how far back we might trace the concept of modern art. While the romantics are a bit too early for our immediate purposes, two figures whose work dates from the middle of the nineteenth century are essential for understanding the main intellectual currents of the following century as they affected novelists.

The German social philosopher Karl Marx (1818–1883) in collaboration with Friedrich Engels (1820–1895) published *The Communist Manifesto* in 1848, the year of European revolutions. Soon afterward Marx went into exile in England, where he produced his multivolume *Das Kapital* between 1867 and 1894, translated into English 1887–1909. Politically, of course, Marx's importance is enormous and can be seen in the establishment of parties and governments, from his disciple Vladimir Lenin's founding of Soviet Russia in 1917 to the growth of British "welfare socialism" and later in the establishment of various third world communist and socialist states. Intellectually, his influence has also been profound. His analysis of society's functioning through social class and his discussion of the alienating effects of modern industrialism on the worker have been dominant concepts even among those who do not share his vision of a dictatorship of the proletariat. Both in England and in America in the twentieth century, intellectuals have been overwhelmingly left-wing in orientation, and during certain periods, such as the 1930s, a substantial number of artists and thinkers were sympathetic to the communist experiment. Marx and Engels's view of literature, which assumes that novels are permeated with ideology — that is, the ideas and values of the ruling class — was influential through the 1930s and again from the 1970s on.

Charles Darwin (1809–1882) is another figure of this stature. Although he was not alone in working out a theory of evolution, his treatise *On the Origin of Species by Means of Natural Selection* (1859) was sufficiently detailed, intellectually authoritative, and firmly founded in direct observation to challenge all competing theories of life on earth, theological or otherwise. *The Descent of Man* (1871) made more explicit Darwin's presumption that human beings share a common descent with all other life forms, thus altering forever the kind of anthropocentric humanism that had descended from the Greek and Roman thinkers and been refigured by the Renaissance. Although Darwin at first was enormously controversial, by the turn of the century it was clear that his thought had carried the day, and adaptations of it were being applied in areas remote from the history of species. Darwin, who had taken training as a minister at Cambridge, insisted that his view of natural selection — survival of the fittest — did not do away with God, although it certainly challenged many varieties of nonconformist and evangelical biblical literalism.

The philosopher Herbert Spencer (1820–1903) found in Darwin's idea of evolution a basic principle that could be used to understand the development of ethics, political systems, psychology, and so forth. Both Spencer's adaptations of Darwin and the popularizations of other writers tended to presume that evolution was goal-directed and progressive. But Darwin's follower Thomas Huxley (1825–1895) in an 1893 lecture specifically attacked Spencer's progressivist interpretation of Darwin, pointing out that the very qualities seen as ethically desirable in humankind may be those that are least effective from the standpoint of brute survival. Along with the popularization of the concept of entropy — the idea in the physical sciences that any closed system moves naturally toward a state of chaos or disorder — Huxley's "dark" Darwinism contributed to a current of intellectual despair around the end of the century. At this time also, the dominant school of thought, formulated by Jean-Baptiste Lamarck (1744–1829) and called Lamarckianism, which had argued that species change occurred in response to conditions — the giraffe's neck lengthening after generations of stretching after leaves — had to give way to the mechanism of random mutation followed by natural selection. This change in the understanding of species change also undermined the presumption of purpose in evolution.

Social Darwinism, the application of the idea of natural selection to social change, especially as it developed in the United States, was most often invoked as a defense of the status quo. After all, the capitalist system was supposed to have established an environment of aggressive competition that mimicked natural competition, and it could be argued that the "casualties" of that competition should, for the betterment of the species, be "selected out." The wealthy Mr. Wilcox, in E. M. Forster's novel *Howards End* (1910), tells his wife in terms much like these that she need not concern herself with the fate of the lower-class Bast family. His wife, like many other intellectuals indirectly influenced by Marx, can see several holes in Wilcox's thinking. For instance, since Wilcox was born middle class and Bast lower class, no "fair competition" has taken place. Like Huxley, one might also challenge the entire Darwinian analogy on moral grounds. When at the end of the novel Forster has Wilcox's self-righteous son kill Bast, he is suggesting that upper-middle-class men live with and suppress considerable rage and fear directed at the underclass. And indeed, the fear of social revolution haunts the American and British middle class throughout the century, from England's fear of "anarchist" atrocities around 1900, portrayed in Conrad's *The Secret Agent* (1907), to the Red scare in the 1950s in the United States and the "culture wars" of the 1960s and 1970s.

A theme common to Darwin and Marx that explains in some degree the opposition to their ideas is mutability, the capacity for change. During his researches, Darwin had written to a friend, "I am almost convinced . . . that species are not (it is like confessing a murder) immutable."[12] Confessing to a belief in the mutability of species was in some ways worse than admitting murder: in America as in Britain, but especially among the Transcendentalists in midcentury America, nature was seen as an available model of divinity. If species were not fixed, then God's pattern dissolved and the natural world was in constant change. Once Mendel's work superseded Lamarck's, moreover, nature was revealed as a randomly shifting flux. In somewhat similar fashion, Marx postulated that societies evolve inevitably over time and that feudal economic systems give way to capitalism and the triumph of the bourgeoisie, which in turn will yield to communism and the rule of the proletariat, finally resulting in a classless utopia. Marx claimed to base his theories on a materialist analysis of labor and capital and to be the pioneer of a genuine science; he stood the idealist Hegel on his head, he claimed, and harnessed the logic of the "dialectic" — Hegel's argument that a "thesis" calls forth its "antithesis" and then a "synthesis" of the two — to material considerations.

Much of Marx's work is cultural analysis, especially analysis of the condition of modernity — what Marxists often call "late capitalism." Marx's diagnosis is that modern industrial society breeds alienation in its workers because they feel removed both from any "organic" pride in production (on an assembly line, no one worker even understands the complete production process) and from the just reward for their labor (much of which goes to the capitalist owners of the means of production). Whether for these reasons or for very different ones, modern writers as various as Ezra Pound and Virginia Woolf, D. H. Lawrence and Sinclair Lewis agreed that the modern condition, especially for the artist, was one of alienation.

The complaint of writers was more likely to be focused on the "philistinism" — the unthinking materialism and lack of interest in a genuine artistic culture — of the British and American middle class. How they related this to the political situation (or, indeed, whether they did so at all) might vary, but most modernist writers at least agreed with Marx's diagnosis. Perhaps the most disturbing and global legacy of both Marx and Darwin was that each man envisioned violent conflict as the natural state of things: for Darwin, conflict was the engine of natural selection, while for Marx class conflict was inevitable until the establishment of the worker's paradise and the disestablishment of the middle class.

A figure whose influence began with the new century and increased at least through the 1950s was the Austrian Sigmund Freud (1856–1939). Freud's first important book, *The Interpretation of Dreams* (1900), posits that the content of dreams is an important though disguised key to the dynamics of a person's psyche; his stress upon the unconscious mind as a repository of the most fundamental drives and his argument that sexual conflicts are embodied in the symbols that arise in dreaming or in free association cast a radically different light on human nature. Freud termed his new method "psychoanalysis," and the first "psychoanalytic congress" was held in 1908. By then the most radical of Freud's ideas were generating controversy in British and European intellectual circles.

In a series of books through the 1930s, Freud elaborated his theories of the Oedipus complex; the division of the self into ego, id, and superego; the mechanisms of repression, projection, introjection, and so forth; and his generalizations of these concepts into theories of the foundation and functioning of societies. His notion that sexuality is a fundamental drive even in childhood and his emphasis on the irrational mechanisms of the unconscious, enormously controversial though they were, at least left most people with a renewed sense of the depth and mystery of human subjectivity. Both Freud and, even more, his erstwhile disciple Carl Jung (1875–1961), in their exploration of symbolism in dream, myth, and literature, suggested that these areas could offer basic knowledge about the workings of the mind. Freud always gave credit to imaginative writers for their insight into the hidden realms that his "science" claimed to illuminate. An implication of the psychoanalytic movement was that imaginative literature was a valuable tool for exploring a reality that empirical science had ignored completely.

If Freud represented a venture into the unknown territory of the mind, Sir James Frazer (1854–1941) — who was otherwise a far less significant figure than Freud — might be said to stand for the British venture into unknown cultures. An approach termed "cultural relativism" was gathering momentum around the turn of the century, reflected both in the preoccupation of artists and writers with "primitive" cultures of Africa and South America and also in the critical, jaundiced eye with which modernists viewed British and American civilization. Frazer's masterpiece of scholarship, *The Golden Bough*, appeared in twelve volumes between 1890 and 1915. A comparative study of magic and religion in a multitude of cultures, it was originally intended to explain the rule regulating the succession of the priesthood of the goddess Diana at Aricia, but gradually grew as Frazer found that he had to address more and more general questions about the logic of magic and belief. Like his later follower Joseph Campbell, Frazer sketched the outlines of a few mythic patterns that can be found in numerous cultures, suggesting the possibility of a science of human societies. A number of modernist writers, such as T. S. Eliot, D. H. Lawrence, H.D., and Ezra Pound, shared an interest in Frazer's discussions of the sacrificed king, the dying god, and the scapegoat; in fact, it was all too easy for European and American artists to identify with such figures.

The influence of the German philosopher and poet Friedrich Nietzsche (1844–1900) is harder to specify, and some philosophers argue that it is only recently beginning to be felt to the fullest extent. His *Birth of Tragedy* (1872) argues against the "Apollonian" interpretation of classical literature that lays emphasis on affirmative values of reason, harmony, and proportion, and affirms a "Dionysian" interpretation that stresses pessimism, passion, and even sexual frenzy. In *Thus Spake Zarathustra* (1883–1892) and *Beyond Good and Evil* (1886) he elaborates the idea of the Übermensch, or Superman, who is morally beyond "herd" ethics. He also rejects Christianity as a "slave morality"; and launches a general attack on empirical science as an interpretation of reality. Nietzsche became well known in Europe following Georg Brandes's lectures on him in Copenhagen in 1888. In that year in a letter he announced the impending "revolution of all values" and declared, "I swear that in two years time the whole world will be in convulsions. I am sheer destiny."[13] Nietzsche's doctrine of the exceptional individual — the Übermensch — had an impact on many early modernists, from G. B. Shaw (1856–1950) to Joyce, Wyndham Lewis, Yeats, Pound, Lawrence, and Hemingway. Some aspects of his thought were taken up by fascist philosophers during the 1930s, though he has also had influence among leftists and anarchists. His attack on so-called objective knowledge sounded a theme that continued throughout the century: "Physics too," he argued, "is only an interpretation and arrangement of the world . . . and *not* an explanation of the world."[14]

ISMS, SCHISMS, AND SCHOOLS

Modernism, unlike most other major literary movements, was represented not by a particular style and structure in literary works, but by the search for an individual style and structure. The major novels of James, Conrad, Joyce, and Faulkner differ tremendously from one another, and the same is true of European modernists like Thomas Mann, Italo Svevo (1861–1928), Marcel Proust, André Gide, Franz Kafka (1883–1924), and Hermann Hesse (1877–1962). The modernist poem could be as short as Pound's and Williams's three-line lyrics or as long and elaborate as Eliot's *The Waste Land*, complete with footnotes. A modernist sentence might be as simple, short, and repetitive as Gertrude Stein's "a rose is a rose is a rose" or as long and complex as some of Faulkner's page-and-a-half declamations in *The Sound and the Fury*. Particularly in the pre–World War I years, modernist art seemed to be headed in several different directions simultaneously; although there was a general agreement among the most vigorous artists that a new direction was called for, there was little consensus about that direction. By now, the fact that modernist art has its own accepted academic canon and rationale tends to disguise the fact that it began as a series of ceaseless avant-garde experiments that constituted an attack on tradition and in some ways on art itself.

Most artists we now call modernist at least agreed about what they did not like. They were tired of old subjects and old artistic forms, and Pound's dictum "Make it new" would be subscribed to by most modernists. In poetry, overthrowing the "tyranny of the iamb," the most common metrical foot, led to the spread of "free verse." In the novel, a multitude of experiments produced fiction with strange or multiple narrators and unusual styles and methods of narration, culminating in the stream of consciousness pioneered by Dorothy Richardson, Woolf, and Joyce and further developed by Faulkner. They also shared an antipathy to middle-class culture, what they saw as crass philistinism and subordination of all other values to commercial ones. In America this feeling was especially acute: H. L. Mencken (1880–1956) pilloried the "Booboisie," and Sinclair Lewis vivisected it in *Babbitt* (1922). Businessmen, however, were unapologetic about their get-up-and-go ethic. The motto of the Chicago Columbian Exposition of 1893 was "Make culture hum!"[15] Modernist artists, on the other hand, rejected the basic premises of industrialism — they recognized no progress in civilization and felt that industrial society was stripping men and women of what was most valuable in them. In some writers, like Theodore Dreiser, this feeling led to political protest as a socialist; in some, like Pound, it led to fascism; while in others, like Lawrence, it was incorporated into a vast, mythic vision of race and gender, creation, and destruction.

Aesthetically, modernists identified the enemy as either Victorianism or romanticism; in any case, most modernists disliked the formless sprawl of many nineteenth-century novels. They abhorred the frequent sentimentalism of Dickens and Thackeray and the sentimental tone of poets like Alfred, Lord Tennyson (1809–1892) as well. Both Joyce and Eliot at times called themselves "classicists." In place of what seemed to them emotional sloppiness, they set an intense concern for form, a characteristic ironic tone, and a "distancing" of the author that they often claimed was "objective" as opposed to the romantics' "subjectivity." Somewhat paradoxically, modernists liked to explore the interiority, the subjectivity of individuals, but they would do so by means of externals; for instance, Eliot's "Love Song of J. Alfred Prufrock" is completely concerned with Prufrock's state of mind but explores it "projectively," by means of external, urban imagery. Modernists are frequently interested in the irrational, the unconscious, the "primitive," and the mythic, although that interest can take many directions: Eliot's use of classical myth as a way of "giving a shape and a significance to the immense panorama of futility and anarchy which is contemporary history"[16] has little in common with, say, the artist Pablo Picasso's (1881–1973) adaptation of some forms of African sculpture.

Modernist art is most notorious for its difficulty, even obscurity. When Edward Albee (b. 1928) titled his play *Who's Afraid of Virginia Woolf?* (1962) he was pointing jokingly to the intellectual challenge of Woolf's writing. "We can only say that it appears likely that poetry in our civilization, as it exists at present, must be difficult," wrote T. S. Eliot.[17] Pound insisted that a serious book of poetry could sell no more than five hundred copies — and, indeed, Wallace Stevens's (1879–1975) *Harmonium* (1923), one of the most important volumes of modern poetry, initially sold less than a hundred copies. Asked why he had written *Finnegans Wake* in such an obscure manner, Joyce replied, "To keep the critics busy for three hundred years." With a smile he told the American writer Max Eastman, "The demand that I make of my reader is that he should devote his whole life to reading my works" — an ideal reader he elsewhere characterized as suffering from "the ideal insomnia."[18]

Some of this is defiant posturing by artists who felt themselves increasingly ignored by the public at large, but some of it springs from a genuinely new and serious view of art. It is linked to the messianic conviction they shared with the Romantic poets before them — the notion that only a nation's best art can save its soul, whether the nation recognizes it or not. Modernist artists have often been accused of elitism, and indeed they can be intellectual elitists. But we should realize that their stance is based in their conviction of art's tremendous importance; it does not necessarily have anything to do with a reader's social position, formal education, gender, or race. While some modernists, like Eliot, had wealthy families and extensive, expensive educations, others, like Woolf and Lawrence, were essentially self-educated. And while some notable modernists were to varying degrees misogynist, racist, or anti-Semitic, some were feminists, most were social progressives, and many welcomed the art of persons who had been socially marginalized. Gertrude Stein, for instance, was enthusiastic about the writing of the African American Richard Wright (1908–1960). Admittedly, this is faint praise; institutional racism was the major reason Harlem Renaissance writers such as Nella Larsen (1891–1964), Jessie Fauset (1886–1961), and Langston Hughes (1902–1967) were not regarded as modernists from the outset (and still are seldom taught in courses on modernism).

Generalizations such as these about modernism are useful, but also dangerous, in that they smooth out quite substantial differences among important artists in the effort to describe a homogeneous literary movement or climate. Critics, for instance, often talk of the doctrine of "authorial impersonality," citing statements by Joyce and Eliot, but then have to deal with the fact that all of Joyce's work is in some way autobiographical, or with Lawrence's writing, which seems in some ways the very opposite of impersonal. If we try to argue that modernist art holds itself above both morality and politics, which it sometimes claims to do, we have to face the fact that no writer is more moralistic than Lawrence, and few writers are more disagreeably political than the later Pound. Because modernists for years were held to be apolitical, Woolf's extensive feminist and political writings were an embarrassment, though now they are among her most widely read works.

Modernism was less a consensus than an interplay of groups, attitudes, and techniques, many of them incompatible. A brief survey of some of the literary movements that contributed to it may be more illuminating than a forced synthesis. Many of the following movements or schools also existed in the graphic arts or music or both. Some were highly programmatic and self-conscious, while others were simply a group of approaches shared by writers working independently and only later given a name by critics. The late nineteenth and early twentieth centuries were times of tremendous ferment, with groups forming, disbanding, splintering, and re-forming under different banners, with different participants. The list that follows artificially simplifies some of that social and artistic flux.

Symbolism

A direct precursor of modernism was the symbolist movement, characterized by aesthetic assumptions among a group primarily composed of
French poets between 1880 and 1895, notably Arthur Rimbaud (1854–
1891) and Stéphane Mallarmé. Charles Baudelaire (1821–1867) was
claimed as a precursor. These poets and their followers believed in sug-
gestion and indirection rather than explicit statement; they conceived of a
further reality beyond the reality of the senses, which could be approached
only in special states of consciousness, such as poetic inspiration, aesthetic reverie, or even (for Rimbaud) "the willed derangement of *all the
senses*" through whatever means.[19] For them the symbol, whose meaning
could not be discursively stated but only indirectly apprehended, was the
key to artistic knowledge. They also frequently employed *synesthesia*, the
deliberate substitution of one sense for another. Mallarmé in particular
affirmed a priesthood of art as an area of mysterious knowledge unappre-
ciated by the uninitiated, especially the bourgeoisie. In Britain an awareness of symbolism was spread by Arthur Symons's book *The Symbolist
Movement in Literature* (1899).

Among novelists, Joyce, Woolf, and Conrad were especially influenced
by the symbolist movement, as were most of the modernist poets except
perhaps William Carlos Williams (1883–1963). In a larger sense, it is arguable that novelists like Hawthorne and Melville were symbolists "before the fact" — or indeed that symbolism has always been an important
artistic technique.

Naturalism

Naturalism was a literary movement pioneered mostly by French writers of fiction in the last third of the nineteenth century (see chap. 1, pp.
13–15). As conceived by Émile Zola, its chief theoretician, naturalism
was an objective, "scientific" treatment of humanity in literature: people,
generally of the lower class — prostitutes, agricultural workers, factory
workers — were presented unsentimentally, at the mercy of their instincts.
Naturalism was clearly a legacy of Darwin, but its tone was usually pessi-
mistic. Zola took pains in researching his milieus and presenting a wealth
of concrete detail; especially in the work of American naturalists like Jack
London (1876–1916), Frank Norris, and Theodore Dreiser, there was often
an element of muckraking journalism. A number of modern writers
adopted the naturalistic technique of objectively presenting details of "low"
experience usually left out of fiction without necessarily subscribing to
the naturalist belief that human life is completely subject to "natural"
laws. There are clear naturalistic elements in the writing of Joyce,

Lawrence, Sherwood Anderson (1876–1941), and Hemingway, different as they are from Zola and from one another. Although naturalism and symbolism in some respects are opposing approaches to literature, innovative writers like Joyce and Crane managed to use both, sometimes within the same work. Readers through the present day have found that their appetite for documentary information and for unsentimental narratives is best satisfied by naturalistic novels; Anne Petry's (b. 1911) naturalistic novel *The Street* (1946), for example, was the first novel by an African American woman to sell more than a million copies. But although painstaking documentation of concrete details of all sorts has become the norm in fiction in this century, "pure naturalism" in Zola's sense died before the turn of the century. One critic has suggested that the movement exhausted itself in inventorying the world while that world was still orderly enough to be inventoried.

Impressionism

While naturalism was, at least in France, a self-conscious movement complete with manifestos, literary impressionism was a vaguely defined set of fictional techniques practiced by a group of writers around the turn of the century (see chap. 1, pp. 13–15). Some of these writers discussed their methods with one another, some did not. If naturalism stressed objective documentation of external facts of the physical world, impressionism emphasized the inward, human, variable perception of things and events — a perception altered radically by point of view, external conditions, and the temperament of the perceiver. In what has been called "delayed decoding," a writer such as Conrad might first present a baffling sensory impression (as when in *Heart of Darkness* Marlow suddenly sees "little sticks" in the air) before allowing the perceiver to understand what is going on (as when Marlow realizes his boat is being attacked by men on the banks shooting arrows). Henry James said that the result in Conrad was "a prolonged hovering flight of the subjective over the outstretched ground of the case exposed."[20] In Joyce, Woolf, and Faulkner it was a remarkable focus on sensory details and on the movements and quality of consciousness itself, especially as presented in stream of consciousness narration.

Expressionism

The term *expressionism* was first coined to distinguish certain tendencies in early-twentieth-century painting from impressionism. The canvases of Vincent van Gogh (1853–1890) and Edvard Munch (1863–1944) in particular, with their violent emotional content and relative indifference

to the technical and formal aspects of painting that had preoccupied the
impressionists, seemed to warrant a separate term. The term *expressionist* was soon applied to several antirepresentational German painters and
to some German drama around 1914–1924. Relatively few British or
American and virtually no French writers were regularly called expressionist, though the term probably best fit Wyndham Lewis, who was a
graphic artist as well as a writer.

  Still, some critics have argued that expressionism is really the common
denominator of most modernist artists. Antirealistic, dreamlike passages
such as the "Nighttown" section of Joyce's *Ulysses*, much of Woolf's
Orlando (1928) and *The Waves* (1931), passages throughout Lawrence,
novels by May Sinclair, Jean Rhys (1894–1979), and Djuna Barnes (1892–
1982), sections of novels of John Dos Passos (1896–1970) and Ralph Ellison
(b. 1914) and the drama of Eugene O'Neill (1888–1953) or even Thornton
Wilder (1897–1975) — all might be called expressionist and have been
more fruitfully approached for their psychological content than for their
formal presentation. Kafka's work has been called expressionist, with its
dreamlike, obsessive settings and irrealistic premises. It is likely that because impressionism presented itself as a form of realism and, in a way
congenial to the New Criticism of American academics, stressed formal
matters, expressionism has been undervalued in the history of the twentieth-century novel. It is also interesting that innovative writing by women
and African Americans in the 1920s can frequently be called expressionist, as can later novels grouped under the rubric of "magic realism." Today, works that earlier might have been termed expressionist are now
routinely called postmodern (see chap. 3).

Imagism

  Imagism was an Anglo-American poetic movement first promoted by
Ezra Pound, who was inspired by T. E. Hulme's (1883–1917) aesthetic
philosophy attacking romanticism and favoring the "hard, dry image." The
first anthology, *Des Imagistes* (1914), included poems by Pound, H.D.,
Richard Aldington (1892–1962), Amy Lowell (1874–1925), William Carlos
Williams, and Ford Madox Hueffer (who later changed his last name to
Ford). D. H. Lawrence contributed to later collections. Imagist principles
included verbal concentration and economy, the use of ordinary, "unpo-
etic" language, the creation of new rhythms (as opposed to regular meters),
the use of "free verse," the availability of any subject matter, and the presentation of images as the essence of the poem. A surprising number of
these principles have characterized twentieth-century poetry through to-

day, and they have had a strong effect on artistic prose as well. Woolf's novels, for instance, can be termed imagist. Unable to control the movement and distracted by other artistic interests, Pound soon abandoned it, contemptuously referring to it as "Amygism" after Amy Lowell assumed leadership.

Futurism

Futurism was an avant-garde movement primarily in Italian art, literature, and music, led by Filippo Marinetti (1876–1944), whose *Futurist Manifesto* (1909) set out some of the movement's principles. Futurists embraced industrial technology, worshiping power and speed, and in their apocalyptic writings looked positively upon virility, nationalism, and war. By the 1930s Marinettti was subsumed by the growing culture of Italian fascism, which also appealed strongly to Pound. Futurists anticipated later avant-garde movements by abandoning traditional syntax, punctuation, and meter in writing; indeed, they were probably the first "performance artists," and often combined different artistic genres in chaotic performances. In a literary context futurism is important mostly as the embodiment of an antihumanist tendency in early modernism, as analyzed most famously in José Ortega y Gasset's (1883–1955) "The Dehumanization of Art" (1925). Ortega argues that the "new sensibility" in modern art denudes objects of their quality of "lived" or "human" reality; and certainly the unsentimental, antiromantic thrust of much modernist art, its emphasis on impersonality, as Eliot put it, has this sort of effect.[21] Images of machinery crop up in some unexpected places, as in William Carlos Williams's observation "A poem is a small (or large) machine made out of words."[22] Some modernists, of course, felt they were true, revolutionary humanists instead and had no sympathy for futurism. Lawrence's *Women in Love* (1920) includes a full-blown attack on the fictional artist Loerke, who seems to be a futurist and a formalist as well.

Vorticism

Vorticism was a movement chiefly in sculpture and art that flourished between 1912 and 1915. Its most notable figures were Wyndham Lewis, Ezra Pound, and the French sculptor Henri Gaudier-Brzeska, who died in World War I. After breaking with futurism, Lewis founded the iconoclastic periodical *Blast* in 1914. Graphically, vorticism borrowed from cubism, in its tendency to represent human figures with abstract planes and angles, almost as if they had exoskeletons. Literary vorticism stressed

energy, an attack on bourgeois culture, and a rather confused mixture of
the numerous ideas of Lewis and Pound. Lewis's vorticist stories are often brutally unsentimental and explore bohemian society with a sharp
and satiric eye for the external appearances of characters. Lewis presented
vorticism in fiction as an alternative to impressionism, which he disliked,
and also as an alternative to what he saw as an obsession with time on the
part of modernist writers, an idea on which he expanded in his polemic
Time and Western Man (1927).

Surrealism

The surrealist movement was founded in Paris in 1924 and explained
in the *Surrealist Manifesto* of its leader, André Breton (1896–1966), that
year. It was announced as a mode of thought with revolutionary implications throughout life, but its most prominent productions were in poetry
and in art (where Joan Miró [1893–1983] and Salvador Dali [1904–1989]
were famous practitioners). Breton's surrealist novel *Nadja* (1928) is still
read, however. Explicitly founded on Freud's theories of the unconscious,
surrealism experimented with poetic production using free association
and other "automatic" processes for generating unexpected images. By
the 1930s several British writers, notably David Gascoyne (b. 1916) and
Herbert Read (1893–1968), had joined the movement, and it had developed a Marxist dimension. Surrealism is less important to the Anglo-American novel as a coherent school than as an influence that can be seen in the
novels of writers as diverse as Nathanael West (1903–1940), John Hawkes
(b. 1925), and Michael Ondaatje (b. 1943). Some of the prose of Gertrude
Stein and of Joyce has been described as surrealist before the fact.

FILM AND THE MODERN NOVEL

At least as important as any literary school in its impact on the modern
novel is film. This new mass medium entered public consciousness in the
early years of the century; its cultural influence in England and America
was substantial by the 1920s and continued to grow in the following decades. Like the novel, film has always been primarily a mode of mass
entertainment suitable for an industrial age, and the two genres share
many similarities. After all, more than half of all films are based on novels
and stories.[23] As mass media critic Marshall McLuhan observed in the
1960s, "It would be difficult to exaggerate the bond between print and
movie in terms of their power to generate fantasy in the viewer or reader."[24]

Novel and film both manage to generate fantasy through a series of narrative conventions, many of them shared. Indeed, if we examine the development of the novel since the mid-nineteenth century, it is almost as if that genre were anticipating the arrival of the movies.

Probably starting with the huge, sprawling comedies of Charles Dickens and the French novelist Honoré de Balzac, the novel became increasingly visual and documentary. During the late nineteenth century, novels by and large dramatized more, offered more dialogue, and relied less on synopsis. They offered fewer philosophical observations by the narrator and more description of apparently random "street furniture," what writers in the twentieth century took to calling "substantiating detail" because the presence of so many *things* not strictly necessary to the plot made a narrative more convincingly real. By 1888, Henry James was praising the French novelist Guy de Maupassant in terms a film director might have welcomed: "His eye *selects* unerringly, unscrupulously, almost impudently — catches the particular thing in which the character of the object or the scene resides, and by expressing it with the artful brevity of a master, leaves a convincing, original picture."[25]

In this process the influence of Flaubert was paramount. Flaubert had pioneered what we might call "cinematic form" in the novel. In a well-known scene at the Agricultural Fair in *Madame Bovary*, Flaubert "intercuts" scenes of Emma being seduced by her aristocratic beau in an upper room of the town hall with scenes of the animals and peasants in the streets, and he counterpoints the banal dialogue of romance with the awarding of prizes for the best manure. Because of the intensive visualization and the ironic juxtaposition of scenes, no subjective comment is necessary. Indeed, throughout the novel Flaubert tends to show character through a mass of environmental detail and trivial action rather than through a narrator's description of someone. In their different ways, impressionists and naturalists extended Flaubert's use of concrete detail and made more programmatic the tendency of the British novel toward documentation and dramatization.

Relatively few cinematic effects have no prose equivalent. The cinematic technique of montage can be suggested in prose by a series of descriptive passages juxtaposed without transitions, as in Joyce. The inclusion in a narrative of chance or adventitious objects, which is almost inevitable in films, is also common in naturalistic writing. Perhaps it is the strictly visual effects that are hardest for prose to evoke: the limited field of view, for instance, the "depthlessness" of the film image, in which equal prominence is given to all objects, or the multiple-exposure techniques pioneered by Soviet director Dziga Vertov (1895–1954). Of course, prose is also unable to match the visceral immediacy of the movies, which in large part have displaced novels as sources of sheer excitement.

The modern writer whose work is most often called cinematic is James Joyce, especially in *Ulysses* (1922). For instance, in the "Wandering Rocks" section of that book he moves rapidly and without transition among a series of scenes in Dublin, all taking place at approximately the same time. On top of that, into each scene Joyce injects brief "interpolations" belonging to other scenes. The famous Russian director Sergei Eisenstein (1898–1948), an admirer of *Ulysses*, met with Joyce in 1930, and the two men's mutual admiration has inspired a good deal of writing about Joyce and the cinema; but Joyce was at best lukewarm to various proposals to film *Ulysses*, and despite his early attempt to set up a chain of movie theaters in Dublin, he seldom went to the cinema.[26]

Aside from Joyce, a good many modern writers have been described as using cinematic effects in their writing, whether or not they were consciously trying to do so. These range from Conrad, Wyndham Lewis, Woolf, and Hemingway through Faulkner, John Steinbeck (1902–1968), and Malcolm Lowry (1907–1957), up to Ken Kesey (b. 1935) and a host of contemporary novelists. There is no sure way to determine influence in a situation like this: Did Faulkner write cinematically because of Flaubert? Because, especially in *The Sound and the Fury*, he was inspired by Joyce? Because he was fascinated by movies? Because a "filmic consciousness" is part of the twentieth-century Zeitgeist, whatever an author's personal interests and feelings may be?

Sometimes we do have external evidence that a writer is consciously attempting some adaptations of film conventions. This is the case for various novels of Aldous Huxley (1894–1963), John Dos Passos, Graham Greene (1904–1991), Wright Morris (b. 1910), Vladimir Nabokov (1899–1977), William Burroughs (b. 1914), and Alain Robbe-Grillet, who is also a screenplay writer and director. Greene's "entertainments" (as he called them), espionage novels like *The Ministry of Fear* (1943), are crafted to evoke an atmosphere of brooding menace, partly in imitation of "noir" films of the 1940s. The espionage novels of Eric Ambler (b. 1909), many written during the 1930s, are heavily filmic — Ambler also wrote screenplays. Dashiell Hammett's (1894–1961) detective thrillers of the same period have long descriptive passages in which every tiny motion or change in appearance of the protagonist is described but his feelings are never discussed.

A more consciously experimental adaptation of film technique is evident in some of the prose of John Dos Passos. Dos Passos visited Russia and was exposed to the work of Eisenstein and Vertov in 1928, while he was writing *The 42nd Parallel*, the first volume of the *U.S.A.* trilogy. Vertov's manifestos entitled *The Camera Eye* may have been the source of the sections with the same title in *U.S.A.*[27] In *The 42nd Parallel*, the "Camera Eye" sections trace the consciousness of a growing boy, mostly through a technique we might term "stream of observation," since the boy's consciousness hardly seems involved:

> O qu'il a des beaux yeux said the lady in the seat opposite but She said that was no way to talk to children and the little boy felt all hot and sticky but it was dusk and the lamp shaped like half a melon was coming on dim red and the train rumbled and . . . the blue tassel bobs on the edge of the dark shade shaped like a melon and everywhere there are pointed curved shadows.[28]

These alternate with "Newsreel" sections that are punctuated by headlines and that rapidly shift from one public event to another. Like Vertov and Eisenstein in their films, Dos Passos refuses to allow a single consciousness to preside over his work. Throughout, he approximates the effect of montage, the rapid succession of scenes without narrative transition, or the superimposition of one image upon another.

Of course, a good number of fiction writers have been directly involved with the making of movies in one way or another. The most surprising of these is probably Rudyard Kipling (1865–1936), who wrote a screenplay for the British Empire Marketing Board. Even as unlikely a propagandist as the Welsh poet Dylan Thomas (1914–1953) wrote screenplays for the British government during World War II, and between the wars Christopher Isherwood (1904–1986) worked on documentaries. Isherwood, whose stories about Berlin are best known to American audiences through the movie *Cabaret*, adopted a tone of almost spooky objectivity in some of his work. "Goodbye to Berlin" opens with the author-narrator looking out a window:

> I am a camera with its shutter gone, quite passive, recording, not thinking. Recording the man shaving at the window opposite and the woman in the kimono washing her hair. Someday, all this will have to be developed, carefully printed, fixed.[29]

Far greater was the number of American writers who went to Hollywood, often in desperate pursuit of the money to be made writing screenplays. Between 1927 and 1940 alone, these included Maxwell Anderson (1888–1959), Robert Benchley (1889–1945), Stephen Vincent Benét (1898–1943), James M. Cain (1892–1977), John Dos Passos, William Faulkner, F. Scott Fitzgerald, John O'Hara (1905–1970), Dorothy Parker (1893–

1967), S. J. Perelman (1904–1979), Booth Tarkington (1869–1946), Nathanael West, and Philip Wylie (1902–1971). For most, the experience of having their writing judged and revised by groups of strangers without aesthetic qualifications was unpleasant; for some, Hollywood with its temptations was disastrous.[30]

One aspect of the discomfort of "serious" novelists in Hollywood was their conviction that they were practitioners of "high art" meretriciously selling their services to purveyors of schlock. This was not a universal feeling — some authors had respect for the film medium and real hopes for producing good work — but it was widespread during the 1940s. Later in the century, as film continued to gather prestige and as "high modernism" waned, what had been seen as an unbridgeable chasm between serious art and popular entertainment narrowed or disappeared altogether. French intellectuals embraced film particularly early, and beginning in the 1940s influential writers such as Jean-Paul Sartre (1905–1980), André Malraux (1901–1976), Jean Cocteau (1889–1963), Alain Robbe-Grillet, and Jean Genet (1910–1986) all were involved in the cinema. Since then, it has become routine for "high culture" figures, including the most respected novelists, to involve themselves in the making of films.

It should be noted that many critics, including the majority of those teaching in film studies programs, regard film as a wholly separate art from literature, with its own separate aesthetic. From their perspective, the progress of film as a genre was retarded by its early dependence on the novel, just as photography's bid to become an art form was retarded by the efforts of early photographers to imitate the effects of painters. Some would argue that film is inherently a more advanced form than the inevitably linear novel — more conducive to postmodern effects and less tied to banal ways of organizing experience. When, as often happens, the "death of the novel" is proclaimed, film (or, more recently, its cousin, video) is usually declared its successor.

TIME AND SPACE

A huge general shift in perception and in consciousness for the Western world heralded the modern century. As the sociologist H. Stuart Hughes observed, "Nearly all students of the last years of the nineteenth century have sensed in some form or another a profound psychological change."[31] Part of this change was the rejection of positivism, which meant abandoning a putatively scientific, anti-metaphysical empiricism. It also meant abandoning the notion of "objectivity" that was linked with conceptions of the universe as a Newtonian mechanism and of human beings as simply more complex machines than most. But one of the more striking features of the period was a fascination with time, space, and (after Einstein) their relationship. Randall Stevenson has pointed out that during the 1920s, time and space became fashionable terminology and a conscious theme among artists and intellectuals.[32] Although it is a simplification, it is not entirely inaccurate to say that the concepts of space and time became "subjectivized" during the early twentieth century. We can even see certain characteristic modernist techniques, such as the frequent use of allusion and of verbal collage, as the result of attempting a radical compression of time within narrative.

The first impetus for this probably came from the French philosopher Henri Bergson (1859–1941), who developed a concept of "duration" (*la durée*) that signified experienced time rather than objective clock time. Indeed, he attacked the latter in a book published in 1899: "Time, conceived under the form of a homogeneous medium, is some spurious concept, due to the trespassing of the idea of space upon the field of pure consciousness."[33] Albert Einstein's special theory of relativity was published in 1905, his general theory in 1915, with its model of a four-dimensional space-time continuum. When the solar eclipse of 1919 confirmed Einstein's predictions, his name became common coinage. By 1922 Bergson was attempting to find parallels between Einstein's ideas and his own.[34] Meanwhile, Bergson's ideas had spread throughout the intellectual community; his lectures had been attended by both Proust and Wyndham Lewis, who was later to attack what he thought was a dangerous artistic preoccupation with "time consciousness" and "subjectivity." Joyce, who had been specifically attacked in Lewis's *Time and Western Man* (1927) as a "time man," riposted in a section of *Finnegans Wake* (1939).

Thomas Kuhn in *The Structure of Scientific Revolutions* speaks of the change from a Newtonian to a relativistic universe as one of the most profound changes in scientific "paradigm" that history offers.[35] *Relativity* or *relativism* became a byword in all things, from cultural relativism to moral relativism. To the less serious this meant a license to abandon rules and standards entirely, which seemed easy enough in the Roaring Twenties. Meanwhile, the more serious saw it as a call to reformulate the basic principles of all fields of knowledge from a new basis. As D. H. Lawrence put it, "Relativity means . . . there is no one single absolute central principle governing the world."[36] And discoveries around the time of Einstein's had their own far-reaching implications. Work by physicists Ernest Rutherford, Neils Bohr, and Max Planck early in the century suggested that the "indivisible" atom is itself composed of a nucleus orbited by electrons, whose position and charge have "quantized" states — electrons might exist at location *a* or location *b,* but nowhere in between.

Only a bit later, in 1927, Werner Heisenberg formulated his uncertainty principle, according to which it is impossible to determine simultaneously both the position and the velocity of an electron, because the very act of observing the particle affects it. Like Einstein's model, in which statements of position and velocity in space must depend upon a stated "frame of reference" (and have no absolute values), Heisenberg's model implies that objective physical knowledge of the sort imagined in the nineteenth century is an illusion. According to quantum theory, it is not even possible to determine whether subatomic particles are waves or particles — sometimes they act like one, sometimes like the other. And when the implications of Einstein's celebrated equation $E = mc^2$ showing how matter can be converted into energy began to sink in, it seemed that uncertainty and ambiguity ruled the physical universe from the subatomic to the cosmic level. The overall implication of these discoveries and hypotheses in physics was that the basic conceptual blocks through which Europeans and Americans were accustomed to viewing the universe — time, space, matter, and energy — and the modes of measurement they were accustomed to using, which were all continuous, were inappropriate to the new paradigm.

It is always dangerous to draw parallels between developments in the sciences and those in the arts, especially when, as with modernism, the developments in the arts can be said to precede those in physics. Still, it is tempting to find analogies between post-Einsteinian physics and novelists' experimentation with radically compressed or rearranged chronology. In fact, space and time in a sense are already interconnected for the novelist. The careful structuring and patterning of modernist novels make them less an art form to be experienced entirely chronologically, as a sequence of events, and more an example of what the critic Joseph Frank calls "spatial form" — a work of art that must be visualized simultaneously in its entirety, as if it were a painting.[37] Similarly, the idea of relativity would appear to be neatly embodied by the sequence of radically different narrators used in such modernist novels as Joyce's *Ulysses,* Faulkner's *The Sound and the Fury,* Joyce Cary's (1888–1957) trilogy on art (1941–1944) climaxing with *The Horse's Mouth,* and Lawrence Durrell's (1912–1990) *Alexandria Quartet* (1957–1960).

But perhaps the most characteristic effect of what Wyndham Lewis calls the new "time consciousness" among artists is the tendency to collapse meaning into an instant of time. Pound's rationale for imagism is that "an 'Image' is that which presents an intellectual and emotional complex in an instant of time."[38] T. S. Eliot agrees, and his notion of the "objective correlative" is quite similar. Novelists tend to be less theoretically inclined; but Hemingway, for instance, explains that his goal is to capture "what really happened" — "the real thing, the sequence of motion and fact which made the emotion and which would be as valid in a year or ten years or, with luck and if you stated it purely enough, always."[39] The idea is most clearly traced to the late-nineteenth-century aesthetician Walter Pater (1839–1894), who argues that art is perceived — and life most fully experienced — in isolated, almost magical instants of intensity; and, before that, the idea derives from Wordsworth's "spots of time" in *The Prelude* (1850).

But the modernists gave the idea a unique coloration. Probably the most influential formulation was Joyce's in the "epiphany," a brief prose passage representing an instant of perception. Virginia Woolf suggests that most of our lives are made up of "non-being," punctuated by brief flashes or "moments of being," which she relates generally to art.[40] Among the most famous embodiments of the idea is Marcel Proust's evocation of the madeleine in his monumental study of time and memory, the novel sequence *À la Recherche du temps perdu* (1913–1927; trans., *Remembrance of Things Past*, 1922–1931). The madeleine is a bit of cake whose taste brings back vividly a period in the narrator's childhood; other sensory signals, such as a wobbling flagstone, have a similar function. In all these cases the idea is that an image or action, rooted in physical sensation, has the capability of encapsulating a larger experience, meaning, or emotion, or some amalgam of all these, that has enormous artistic significance. The artist's role is to capture, create, or re-create such moments, in which a special, nondiscursive kind of knowledge is imparted.

Of course it is not coincidental that the focus of these writers should be internal, unlike that of their Victorian predecessors. It is in the mind that Bergson's *la durée* is experienced, and in the mind that vast stretches of experience can be encapsulated into an image or a verbal formula. In the twentieth century, the artist's mind for the first time takes on sole responsibility for making the chaos of experience cohere. When Joyce abandoned the draft of his autobiographical novel entitled *Stephen Hero* and refashioned it as *A Portrait of the Artist as a Young Man*, the most striking difference in the latter book is that instead of attempting to represent the entirety of Stephen's childhood and adolescence, Joyce now relies on brief, symbolically charged incidents. The effect is a sort of novelistic synecdoche in which a small part stands for the whole. There is no attempt to make the passage of events in the book mirror the passage of "clock time" in the external world.

And perhaps there is a political thrust to this seizing of time. One of modernism's most arresting images occurs in Fritz Lang's film *Metropolis* (1926), in which a future world-city has most of the populace enslaved to huge machines of production. At one point the protagonist must grasp the hands of what looks like a giant clock and move them rapidly to different positions. At the mercy of this giant mechanism, he appears to be crucified on a clock face. Perhaps by internalizing time and making it the vehicle of the moment of artistic knowledge, the modernists hoped to disengage themselves from the most intimate aspect of industrial control.

NOTES

1. Quoted in Larzer Ziff, *The American 1890s: Life and Times of a Lost Generation* (New York: Viking, 1966) 19.

2. John Stevenson, *British Society, 1914–1945* (London: Penguin, 1984) 22.

3. Filippo Marinetti, "Destruction of Syntax — Imagination without Strings — Words-in-Freedom" (1913), *Futurist Manifestos,* ed. Umbro Apollonio (London: Thames, 1973) 96.

4. Virginia Woolf, "Mr. Bennett and Mrs. Brown" (1923), *A Bloomsbury Group Reader*, ed. S. P. Rosenbaum (Cambridge: Blackwell, 1993) 235.

5. Virginia Woolf, quoted in Randall Stevenson, *Modernist Fiction: An Introduction* (New York: Harvester, 1992) 61.

6. Jacques Derrida, "Structure, Sign, and Play in the Discourse of the Human Sciences, *The Languages of Criticism and the Sciences of Man: The Structuralist Controversy,* ed. Richard Macksey and Eugenio Donato (Baltimore: Johns Hopkins UP, 1970) 249–50.

7. Dorothy Richardson, *Pilgrimage,* vol. 2 (New York: Knopf, 1967) 99.

8. Paul Fussell, *The Great War and Modern Memory* (New York: Oxford UP, 1975) 8.

9. Ernest Hemingway, *A Farewell to Arms* (New York: Scribner's, 1969) 184–85.

10. Eric J. Hobsbawm, *An Age of Extremes: A History of the World, 1914–1991* (New York: Pantheon, 1994) 179.

11. On the exclusion of women from the modernist canon, see Sandra Gilbert and Susan Gubar, *No Man's Land: The Place of the Woman Writer in the Twentieth Century,* vol. 1, *The War of the Words* (New Haven: Yale UP, 1988), vol. 2, *Sexchanges* (New Haven: Yale UP, 1989). See also Bonnie Kime

Scott, *The Gender of Modernism: A Critical Anthology* (Bloomington: Indiana UP, 1990).

12. Darwin to Joseph Hooker, 1844, quoted in Cynthia Eagle Russett, *Darwin in America: The Intellectual Response, 1865–1912* (San Francisco: Freeman, 1976) 7.

13. Quoted in James MacFarlane, "The Mind of Modernism," *Modernism, 1890–1930,* ed. Malcolm Bradbury and James MacFarlane (London: Penguin, 1976) 78.

14. Friedrich Nietzsche, *Beyond Good and Evil,* trans. R. J. Hollingdale (1886; Harmondsworth: Penguin, 1990) 44.

15. Eric Homberger, "Chicago and New York: Two Versions of American Modernism," *Modernism: 1890–1930* 151.

16. T. S. Eliot, *"Ulysses,* Order, and Myth," *Selected Prose,* ed. Frank Kermode (New York: Harcourt, 1975) 178.

17. T. S. Eliot, "The Metaphysical Poets," *Selected Prose* 65.

18. All three passages from Richard Ellmann, *James Joyce,* rev. ed. (New York: Oxford UP, 1982) 703.

19. Arthur Rimbaud to Georges Izambard, 13 May 1871, *Rimbaud: Complete Works, Selected Letters,* ed. Wallace Fowlie (Chicago: U of Chicago P, 1966) 303.

20. Quoted in Michael H. Levenson, *A Genealogy of Modernism: A Study of English Literary Doctrine, 1908–1922* (Cambridge: Cambridge UP, 1984) 22. From "The New Novel," *Notes on Novelists: With Some Other Notes* (London: Dent, 1914) 276.

21. José Ortega y Gasset, "First Installment on the Dehumanization of Art," *Contemporary Literary Criticism: Modernism through Poststructuralism,* ed. Robert Con Davis (New York: Longmans, 1986) 34. For Eliot on impersonality, see, for example, "Tradition and the Individual Talent," *Contemporary Literary Criticism* 29–31.

22. Quoted in Hugh Kenner, *A Homemade World: The American Modernist Writers* (New York: Knopf, 1975) 55.

23. Geoffrey Wagner, *The Novel and the Cinema* (Rutherford: Fairleigh Dickinson UP, 1975) 27.

24. Marshall McLuhan, *Understanding Media: The Extensions of Man,* rev. ed. (New York: New American Library, 1964) 249.

25. Henry James, "Guy de Maupassant" (1888), quoted in Alan Spiegel, *Fiction and the Camera Eye: Visual Consciousness in Film and the Modern Novel* (Charlottesville: UP of Virginia, 1976) 4.

26. Richard Ellmann, *James Joyce,* rev. ed. (New York: Oxford UP, 1982) 654.

27. Carol Shloss, *In Visible Light: Photography and the American Writer, 1840–1940* (New York: Oxford UP, 1987) 149.

28. Johns Dos Passos, *The 42nd Parallel* (Boston: Houghton, 1946) 27–28.

29. Christopher Isherwood, "A Berlin Diary," *Goodbye to Berlin* (1939; London: Hogarth, 1966) 13.

30. See Richard Fine, *Hollywood and the Profession of Authorship, 1928–1940* (Ann Arbor: UMI Research, 1985) 160–61. Ironically, the horror and despair of the Hollywood experience is probably best captured by Ethan and Joel Coen's film *Barton Fink* (1991), although Nathanael West's surreal novel *The Day of the Locust* (1939) is also powerful testimony.

31. H. Stuart Hughes, *Consciousness and Society: The Reorientation of European Social Thought, 1890–1930* (New York: Knopf, 1958) 34.

32. Randall Stevenson, *Modernist Fiction: An Introduction* (New York: Harvester, 1992) 10.

33. Quoted in Stevenson 103. Henri Bergson, *Time and Free Will: An Essay on the Immediate Data of Consciousness*, trans. F. L. Pogson (London: Allen, 1971) 98.

34. Stevenson 108.

35. Thomas S. Kuhn, *The Structure of Scientific Revolutions*, 2nd ed. (Chicago: U of Chicago P, 1970).

36. D. H. Lawrence, *Fantasia of the Unconscious.* Quoted in Stevenson 71.

37. See Joseph Frank, "Spatial Form in Modern Literature" (1945), *The Widening Gyre* (New Brunswick: Rutgers UP, 1963) 3–62.

38. Ezra Pound, "A Retrospect," *Literary Essays of Ezra Pound,* ed. T. S. Eliot (London: Faber and Faber, 1954) 4.

39. Ernest Hemingway, *Death in the Afternoon* (New York: Scribner's, 1947) 2.

40. Virginia Woolf, *Moments of Being: Unpublished Autobiographical Writings* (New York: Harcourt, 1976) passim.

3

From Modernism
to Postmodernism

What happened in literature after modernism? There is no critical consensus as to the answer to this — nor, indeed, is there a consensus as to whether we are in fact "after modernism" today, despite the proliferation of essays with provocative titles like "What Was Modernism?" and "When Was Modernism?"[1] At least since the 1960s some critics have proclaimed the arrival of a new form of writing (and of the other arts as well), although the term *postmodernism* was not consistently used for this event until the 1970s.[2] Other critics insist that we are still working out the modernist project and that what some people call postmodern is only an exaggeration of certain typically modernist characteristics. Further, we must keep in mind that the great bulk of novels published today, just as in 1922, are standard examples of realism, neither modernist nor postmodern. And there is also the question of how we are to classify "genre" fiction such as science fiction or espionage novels, which the critics who first promoted modernism generally dismiss as subliterary, but which critics sympathetic to postmodernism often see as no different from texts within the literary canon.

Special problems attend the project of writing contemporary literary history. Partly this is because we have no historical perspective on the situation, while the rate of social and historical change seems to be accelerating. It is also possible that modernism itself is not a movement comparable to romanticism, but a disparate bundle of aesthetic tendencies that resist historicizing: modernism's constant demand for novelty, for instance, will necessarily lead to a series of very different works over time. Standard guides to literary history often seem baffled when they come to the twentieth century. The *Pelican Guide to English Literature,* for example, changes its format from broad essays on aspects of writing in previous centuries to short essays on individual modern writers.[3] Still, with these complications in mind, we can attempt a thumbnail sketch of the history of the novel in the twentieth century.

1900–1920

In the novel per se, most of the examples of full-blown modernism during the first two decades of the century are British, perhaps because for British authors the French example was readier to hand; in America the earlier part of the period was mostly distinguished by an American variety of naturalism, often combined with muckraking journalism. Jack London, Theodore Dreiser, Frank Norris, Ellen Glasgow, and Edith Wharton (1862–1937) were at their best. William Dean Howells (1837–1920), America's best-known "man of letters" in the late nineteenth century, was in the twilight of his career, and Henry James's fiction was in its final phase. Regional novels appeared at all points of the literary spectrum, from Willa Cather's (1873–1947) *O Pioneers!* (1913), Sherwood Anderson's erotically charged *Winesburg, Ohio* (1919) and Hamlin Garland's (1860–1940) *Son of the Middle Border* (1917) to Zane Grey's (1875–1939) classic western *Riders of the Purple Sage* (1912). Gertrude Stein's mildly experimental *Three Lives* (1909) featured the voice of an African American woman. American writing took on a new self-consciousness and was rewarded by the publication of the *Cambridge History of American Literature* (1917–1920). In America, one of the modernist battles concerned whether the new kind of writing emerging would be international (as Eliot argued), specifically American (as William Carlos Williams argued), or somehow both (as Pound implied).

In England, H. G. Wells, John Galsworthy, and Arnold Bennett (three writers mocked by Virginia Woolf in her famous essay "Mr. Bennett and Mrs. Brown") were all active, with Bennett and Galsworthy solidly in the realist tradition and Wells specializing in the "novel of ideas" and in science fiction. Rudyard Kipling was coming into his prime, and Thomas Hardy was publishing his last novels, both writers depending to an extent on regional appeal. Among writers sometimes counted as modernists, Joseph Conrad, Ford Madox Ford, and E. M. Forster were all active —

though Forster's early novels were not formally experimental. Dorothy Richardson and May Sinclair developed the stream of consciousness novel in the 1910s, while the modernist short story in English was launched with Katherine Mansfield's *In a German Pension* (1911) and James Joyce's *Dubliners* (1914). D. H. Lawrence and Joyce began publishing just before World War I, and Joyce's *A Portrait of the Artist as a Young Man*, which some think the first fully modernist novel in English, appeared in 1916.

THE 1920s

In America, the Roaring Twenties were announced by F. Scott Fitzgerald's best-selling portrait of "flappers" and their boyfriends, *This Side of Paradise* (1920), and despite Prohibition, the Fitzgeralds' lifestyle of alcohol and conspicuous consumption set the tone of the period. Fitzgerald's *The Great Gatsby* (1925) and Ernest Hemingway's *The Sun Also Rises* (1926) were soon acclaimed as masterpieces; Hemingway's book, set among expatriates in Europe, testified to the remarkable number of American artists who resided in Europe, especially Paris, during the decade. Living was cheap for Americans "following the dollar" around Europe, and alcohol was freely available. Hemingway, who apprenticed himself to Stein, Joyce, and Ford at various points, was a prime example of the internationalizing of American writing in the 1920s. Even William Faulkner at the beginning of his career looked to European masters like Stéphane Mallarmé and brought Joyce's *Ulysses* along on his honeymoon. His own masterpieces of variable point of view, *The Sound and the Fury* (1929) and *As I Lay Dying* (1930), closed the decade. John Dos Passos also spent time in Europe and produced notable experiments in form, including *Three Soldiers* (1921) and *Manhattan Transfer* (1925).

Meanwhile, the Harlem Renaissance was a period of extraordinary creative ferment in the arts generally, including music, dance, and theater, as well as writing in every genre, so that singling out the achievement of the novel alone seems an artificial exercise. The period brought to prominence poets of the quality of Countee Cullen and Langston Hughes, and writers such as Jean Toomer (1894–1967), author of the multigenre work *Cane* (1923), and James Weldon Johnson (1871–1938), a respected older figure who worked in many literary genres. Jamaican-born Claude McKay (1890–1948) published the novels *Home to Harlem* (1928) and *Banjo* (1929), while Jesse Fauset, Nella Larsen, and Johnson's secretary Walter White (1893–1955) during and just after the 1920s all produced novels reflecting the life of the "New Negro." The vogue for "colored" culture among white artists, especially in America, contributed to a broadening of the modernist sensibility and produced some fascinating if embarrassing examples of white artists attempting to use "black material," such as Carl Van Vechten's *Nigger Heaven* (1926).

British fiction in the period was dominated by Lawrence and Woolf, who published throughout the decade, and by Joyce's *Ulysses* (1922). Meanwhile, Aldous Huxley's biting satires *Crome Yellow* (1921) and *Antic Hay* (1923) chronicled the decade's gaiety and loss of moral bearings. His more serious and more formally inventive *Point Counter Point* (1928) borrowed the idea of musical structure from the French novelist André Gide. On the whole, British modernist authors were in closer touch with Continental developments in the arts. Those who lived in Europe at least part of the time often did so because of the freer manners and morals: Joyce raised a family with a woman he had not married, Ford lived with several women while unable to obtain a divorce from his first wife, Wyndham Lewis had a succession of mistresses, and Lawrence was living with a German woman. The moral experimentation of modernist writers was mirrored in their lives, but only the relatively wealthy Bloomsbury group surrounding Virginia Woolf had the social confidence to conduct their notorious affairs on British soil.

THE 1930s

Haunted by the widespread misery in the wake of the stock market crash of 1929, this decade is generally characterized as "political," meaning "leftist," though the influence of Freud was nearly as prominent as that of Marx. In America, John Dos Passos's *U.S.A.* trilogy (1930, 1932, 1936) attacked the degeneration of character in a cynically capitalist America during the first three decades of the century; the ideological slant was formally reinforced by Dos Passos's refusal to focus on a single group of protagonists. Sinclair Lewis's works became even more politically focused after he won the Nobel Prize in 1930, and *It Can't Happen Here* (1935) warned of a fascist revolt in the United States. The rise of fascism and its conflict with socialism in the Spanish Civil War (1936) attracted many intellectuals to the left, and some volunteered for the Spanish Republicans. John Steinbeck's works became increasingly novels of protest, culminating in *The Grapes of Wrath* (1929), which follows a family of "Okies" who leave the Oklahoma dust bowl for California. Meanwhile, a "southern Gothic" strain of fiction, ripe with decadence and sexual obsessions, was explored by Faulkner and by Erskine Caldwell (1903–1987). Shocking as Caldwell's *Tobacco Road* (1932) may have been, Henry Miller (1891–1980) in Paris was testing the boundaries between art and pornography still further with *Tropic of Cancer* (1934). The decade ended with the emergence of the first internationally well-known African American novelist, Richard Wright, in his prize-winning story collection *Uncle Tom's Children* (1938) and his novel *Native Son* (1940) — a book in which both sexual obsession and political protest figure prominently. Wright had given very qualified praise to another writer during this decade, one who had to await critical rediscovery until the 1970s. This was the anthropologist Zora Neale Hurston (1903–1960), whose masterpiece *Their Eyes Were Watching God* (1937) broke new ground in the exploration of voice in the novel.

In England, the tone of the 1930s was set by the trio of young poets W. H. Auden (1907–1973), Stephen Spender (1909–1995), and C. Day-Lewis (1904–1992), all socially committed leftist intellectuals who tried to forge a modernist poetry that demonstrated political commitment during what Auden characterized as a "low, dishonest decade." Most of the period's best narrative prose is not found in the mainstream realist novel. Aldous Huxley's *Brave New World* (1932) explored possible future consequences of genetic manipulation of humans in a world state. Christopher Isherwood specialized in documentary narratives, while George Orwell (1903–1950) (the pseudonym of Eric Blair, chosen for its working-class associations) produced factual stories of his experiences among the lower classes in *Down and Out in Paris and London* (1933) and *The Road to Wigan Pier* (1937). Eric Ambler's leftist thrillers established a pattern for later literate spy novelists such as John Le Carré (b. 1931) and, perhaps because of their cinematic qualities, have worn better than many mainstream novels of the period.

Orwell was typical of the decade in saying that although his admiration of Joyce, Eliot, and their generation was not unqualified — he especially abhorred Yeats's flirtation with fascism and Pound's embrace of it — he respected the fact that they broke out of the insular "cultural circle in which England had existed for something like a century" and "brought back the sense of history."[4] Graham Greene, who was prolific during both the 1930s and 1940s, alternated between symbolic melodramas, a type of thriller he called an "entertainment," and serious novels dealing darkly with crises of faith in Catholicism. Evelyn Waugh (1903–1966), like Greene a Catholic convert, began in the late 1920s producing bitter social comedies, climaxing in the bizarre *Ordeal of Gilbert Pinfold* in 1957. A writer far more experimental than these is the Irishman Brian O'Nolan (1911–1966), who wrote under the name Flann O'Brien. His *At Swim-Two-Birds* (1939), which was praised by Joyce, was later hailed as a comic masterpiece of postmodernism.

THE 1940s

The war years, 1939–1945, interrupted much literary production, as many writers were employed in broadcasting or in writing propaganda, if they were not on active duty. Critics speak of a "neoromantic" quality to the decade, examplified in the word-drunk outpourings of Thomas Wolfe (1900–1938) in *You Can't Go Home Again* (1940) or the poetry and prose of the Welsh poet, story writer, and memoirist Dylan Thomas (1914–1953), the most famous literary figure of the decade. With *For Whom the Bell Tolls* (1940), set in the Spanish Civil War, Hemingway recaptured much of his earlier form, and Faulkner continued to produce substantial novels. The Southern Renaissance, which produced critics such as Cleanth Brooks (b. 1906), John Crowe Ransom (1888–1974), and Allen Tate (1899–1979) — and thus greatly contributed to the New Criticism — during the 1920s and 1930s, began to produce distinguished fiction such as Eudora Welty's (b. 1909) *Delta Wedding*, Robert Penn Warren's (1905–1989) *All the King's Men*, and Carson McCullers's (1917–1967) *Member of the Wedding* (all in 1946). Norman Mailer's (b. 1923) *The Naked and the Dead* (1948) introduced a major voice of the 1950s and 1960s and the first serious novel of World War II.

The 1940s were equally difficult to characterize in England. Perhaps the finest novelist of the decade was Elizabeth Bowen (1899–1973), a less experimental heir to Virginia Woolf who had also written during the previous decade, notably *The Death of the Heart* (1938). In *The Heat of the Day* (1949) she wrote one of the best "domestic" novels about the war. Bowen's friend Rosamond Lehmann (b. 1901) also wrote intriguing lyrical novels during the decade, as did Ivy Compton-Burnett (1892–1969), whose unusual narratives consist almost entirely of dialogue. George Orwell's best-known books, *Animal Farm* (1945) and *Nineteen Eighty-Four* (1949), appeared late in the period. A writer better known to other writers than to the public was Henry Green (1905–1973) (a pseudonym for the industrialist Henry Yorke). Starting in the 1920s, Green published novels, many employing an unusually colloquial style and tight formal design. *Loving* (1945) is among his most admired works.

THE 1950s AND 1960s: THE RISE OF THE POSTMODERN

Most accounts of postmodernism locate a break in sensibility following World War II, and some critics point to the dropping of the atomic bomb in 1945 and the commencement of the "nuclear age" as a defining moment. These accounts date from the 1960s and 1970s and sometimes cite works as far back as Kafka's "The Metamorphosis" (1916; trans., 1937) or Alfred Jarry's (1873–1907) violent farce *Ubu Roi* (1896). But most early accounts take as benchmarks such fiction as J. D. Salinger's (b. 1919) *Catcher in the Rye* (1951), Saul Bellow's (b. 1915) *Adventures of Augie March* (1953), Jack Kerouac's (1922–1969) *On the Road* (1957), Joseph Heller's (b. 1923) *Catch-22* (1961), and William Burroughs's monument of socially transgressive and formally inventive writing, *Naked Lunch* (1964); poetry like Allen Ginsberg's (b. 1926) *Howl* (1956); and drama in the line of Samuel Beckett's (1906–1989) *Waiting for Godot* (1952; trans., 1955) as well as his narrative trilogy *Molloy*, *Malone Dies*, and *The Unnameable* (1951–1953; trans., 1951–1960). Clearly the keynote among these mostly American works is disillusionment, sometimes alleviated by an anarchic joy. An important figure who does not easily fit this context is the Georgia author Flannery O'Connor (1925–1964), whose short stories and novels — among them *Wise Blood* (1952) and *The Violent Bear It Away* (1960) — testify to a modern Gothic sensibility and a Catholic perspective even darker than that of her British contemporary Graham Greene.

The 1950s witnessed a great deal of talk about the alienation of various social groups from the mainstream American middle class and the rise of juvenile delinquency chronicled in movies like *The Wild One* (1954) and *Rebel without a Cause* (1955). Both delinquency and the Beat subculture of free-form jazz, drugs, and coffee-house anarchists were thought to be related to the pessimism and anomie expressed by French existentialist writers, notably Jean-Paul Sartre in *Nausea* (1938; trans., 1949) and Albert Camus (1913–1960) in *The Stranger* (1942; trans., 1946). Perhaps the finest American novel of the decade, Ralph Ellison's *Invisible Man* (1952), combined naturalism with nearly surreal passages; the alienation of the protagonist was as extreme as anything in Beckett but was clearly grounded historically in his plight as an African American. In *Giovanni's Room* (1956) James Baldwin (1924–1987) added to that the cultural estrangement felt by a gay African American.

In England the cultural currents moved somewhat differently. There postwar disillusionment took the form of protest against the remnants of the British class system through a group of writers termed by journalists the Angry Young Men. Notable works by this group included Kingsley Amis's (1922–1995) *Lucky Jim* (1954), John Wain's (b. 1925) *Hurry on Down* (1953), John Braine's (1922–1986) *Room at the Top* (1957), and John Osborne's (b. 1929) drama *Look Back in Anger* (1956). The group's social protest, however pointed, was never as profound as that of the Beats, and none of the Angries had a taste for formal experimentation anything like that of William S. Burroughs with his "cut-up" method of randomly juxtaposing passages of writing from different contexts.

Indeed, the Angry Young Men gradually emerged as culturally conservative antimodernists. Philip Larkin (1922–1985), the chief poet of the generation, argued that literary modernism was an artistic cul-de-sac, an artificial, American-inspired detour from the main line of British poetry. Some British novelists, like William Golding (b. 1911) in *Lord of the Flies* (1954), presented an existentially bleaker picture than the Angries did, but at the time few seemed interested in continuing the modernist project. Many, like C. P. Snow (1905–1980) and Anthony Powell (b. 1905), wrote large novel-sequences of considerable interest that made minimal use of modernist techniques. Lawrence Durrell and Joyce Cary, with their novel-sequences employing shifting points of view, might be called late-modernist exceptions. In a different way, so is Iris Murdoch (b. 1919), whose *Under the Net* (1954), with its mild surrealism, farcical action, and deliberately flat characters, is sometimes claimed for postmodernism.

EARLY CRITICS OF THE POSTMODERN

Among the first critics to herald what they saw, in different ways, as a departure in the arts were Susan Sontag in her 1964 essay "Against Interpretation," Ihab Hassan in "The Dismemberment of Orpheus" (1963), and Leslie Fiedler in "The New Mutants" (1965). By 1966 there had been enough discussion of the as yet unnamed departure that critic Frank Kermode thought it worthwhile to point out that the tendencies signaled by these critics were not inconsistent with modernism.[5] Hassan's early work stresses the idea of a literature of silence and antiformalism whose greatest representative is Beckett; Sontag also evokes a kind of silence, in that the films she discusses, notably those of Jean-Luc Godard (b. 1930) and Alain Robbe-Grillet and Alain Resnais's (b. 1922) *Last Year at Marienbad*, in her view radically resist interpretation. Sontag's call for a new artistic authenticity and sensuous immediacy without regard to meaning leads her to champion antirepresentational art of the 1960s such as Robert Rauschenberg's (b. 1925) paintings.

Where Sontag remains interested in form (or the attack on "high" art, Fiedler prefers to promote a new personal stance towaᵣᵤ ture. He hails the new "barbarians" whom he sees as the representatives of an apocalyptic future — more "Black than White," as he phrases it — to prepare for a "post-humanist, post-male, post-white, post-heroic world."[6] In a slightly later essay, "Cross the Border — Close the Gap: Post-Modernism," Fiedler acclaims a non-highbrow, antirational, apocalyptic sensibility, the alienated stance of the Beats and of writers like Norman Mailer. The new art, he predicts, will turn high art into a burlesque by incorporating elements from science fiction, the western, even pornography, and will abandon representationalism. Fiedler, whose focus is on contemporary American art and the emerging counterculture of the 1960s, is suggesting something like a native alternative to the Enlightenment tradition that will be populist and politically progressive as well as anarchic and sensually Dionysian.

In several publications around 1971 Ihab Hassan tries to establish a "tradition" of the postmodern both within and preceding modernism itself, including figures such as Jarry, Kafka, de Sade, and the surrealist Breton, as well as more contemporary postwar figures who might fit a "period" definition of postmodernism. He offers a long series of suggestive oppositions between modernism and postmodernism: form vs. antiform; purpose vs. play; design vs. chance; hierarchy vs. anarchy; mastery/logos vs. exhaustion/silence; art object vs. process; presence vs. absence; centering vs. dispersal; genre vs. text; signified vs. signifier; readerly vs. writerly; genital/phallic vs. polymorphous/androgynous; determinacy vs. indeterminacy; and many more. The list reflects some of the ideas developed by Hassan, Fiedler, and Sontag during the period. Other elements reflect an influential essay by the American novelist John Barth called "The Literature of Exhaustion" (1967), in which he argues that the modernist project played most of the changes possible in literature, leaving the contemporary writer in extremis. Concentrating on the Argentine Jorge Luis Borges (1899–1986), he sees in that writer a recognition that there is no real "originality" in literature, but "all writers are more or less faithful . . . translators and annotators of pre-existing archetypes."[7]

Still others of Hassan's terms (*text, signified, writerly*) suggest the influence of the French theorist Roland Barthes, whose critical formulations began to be felt in America in the late 1960s (see chap. 1). This influence is especially important because, in the same way that modernism can be said to have generated a critical language (the New Criticism) to analyze and validate itself, postmodernism became associated with — and championed by — the European critical approaches known (in order of their arrival) as the *nouvelle critique,* structuralism, and post-structuralism. And just as discussions of the modern in the arts gave place to sociological and philosophical discussions of modernity as a condition, discussion of postmodern literature, art, architecture, music, and so forth has given way to discussions of what critic Jean-François Lyotard has termed "the postmodern condition."

The influx of European theory probably began with Alain Robbe-Grillet's *For a New Novel* (1963; trans., 1965), an aesthetic polemic meant to defend and explain the French "nouveau roman" (new novel) of Robbe-Grillet, Michel Butor (b. 1926), Nathalie Sarraute (b. 1902), and others. Robbe-Grillet's stance was antihumanist, and he defended his novels' concentration on objects, refusal to portray consciousness continuously, and lack or disruption of linear plot as an aesthetic advance for the novel. A more lasting contribution to the idea of a contemporary novel was made by Barthes, who held up the "new novel" as an example of a "text" (the word *work* or *novel* had too humanist a connotation) that was "writerly" rather than "readerly" (engaged the reader in creative interaction instead of playing to his or her outworn expectations) and "modern" rather than "classic" (although Barthes seemed to mean "contemporary" or "experimental" rather than "modernist" by this term). Barthes and other structuralists claimed to derive their principles from the linguist Ferdinand de Saussure, who distinguished between the verbal "signifier" (a linguistic unit) and its "signified" (which is arbitrary and always absent). Structuralists stress the systemic freedom of the former and, in a revolutionary move, grant no priority to the latter. Just as this phase of European critical theory was preeminently language-based, its aesthetic, which gradually became associated with concepts of postmodernism, heavily stressed verbal autonomy, narrative form, and experimentation — characteristics of writing that highlight the functions of language and of narrative.

While European writers had an enormous influence on the development of the modern novel in Britain, American novelists on the whole paid them less attention, and after the high-water mark of modernism in the 1920s they seemed still less interested in international writing than before. This changed completely in the late 1960s, as a group of non-Anglophone writers became major influences on American novelists even more than on British ones. Indeed, the entire British/American division in literary studies began to make less sense as writers in both countries responded to the work of one another and as Anglophone writers from Canada, New Zealand, Australia, the Caribbean, and various African countries began to make their presence felt (see chap. 4). Aside from the Irishman Beckett, who wrote in French as well, among the earliest such influences were Jorge Luis Borges, whose self-reflexive fictions were widely read in translation, and the Russian émigré writing in English named Vladimir Nabokov, whose scandalous *Lolita* (1955) was followed by a "novel" entitled *Pale Fire* (1962) in which a poem by a fictional poet is endlessly and madly explicated by a fictional academic.

A temporary consensus vision of the postmodern began to emerge in the 1970s, in which the stress was on reflexivity — fictions in some way *about* fiction, which might involve formal experimentation, radical refusal of realistic mimesis, parody, experiments in stylistics, and more. The terms *metafiction* and *surfiction,* designating different strains of reflexivity, came into common usage.[8] John Barth's *The Sot-Weed Factor* (1960) and *Giles Goat-Boy* (1966) were exemplary. The former, a fictional gloss on a real eighteenth-century poem by Ebeneezer Cook, is a picaresque adventure set in the late seventeenth century and narrated in the style of an eighteenth-century novel. The latter is a kind of allegory of life on the Campus, featuring a protagonist who is a cross between human and goat and another who is a computer.

The most frequently cited postmodern author has probably been Thomas Pynchon (b. 1937), especially his early novels *V.* (1963), *The Crying of Lot 49* (1966), and *Gravity's Rainbow* (1973), all of which thematize a sort of cosmic cultural paranoia. Other names to be reckoned with in postmodern American fiction include Kurt Vonnegut, Jr. (b. 1922), William Gass (b. 1924), Robert Coover (b. 1932), and Donald Barthelme (1931–1989) — all fantasists to some degree. "New wave" science fiction attracted critical attention, and some welcomed its more literary practitioners, including Samuel Delany (b. 1942), Ursula K. Le Guin (b. 1929), and the British J. G. Ballard (b. 1930). Since the 1970s a host of brilliant woman writers of science fiction (in this new broader sense) have emerged, including the African American Octavia Butler (b. 1947), while "mainstream" authors like the Rhodesian Doris Lessing (b. 1919) have sometimes crossed over to use the genre experimentally. In England, John Fowles (b. 1926) whose *French Lieutenant's Woman* (1969) mimicked a Victorian novel but featured intrusive comments and appearances by a figure named John Fowles, was often included in this group, as was Angela Carter (1940–1992) with her hallucinatory fables such as *Nights at the Circus* (1984).

In a companion piece to his earlier essay, Barth in "The Literature of Replenishment" (1980) speaks as a leading postmodernist coming to terms with the word. "My ideal postmodernist author neither merely repudiates nor merely imitates either his twentieth-century modernist parents or his nineteenth-century premodernist grandparents. He has the first half of the century under his belt, but not on his back," writes Barth.[9] He points to the foreign authors he has heard termed postmodernist: aside from Borges, Beckett, and Nabokov, he mentions in particular Italo Calvino (1923–1985), Gabriel García Márquez (b. 1928), Julio Cortázar (1914–1984), as well as the French "new novelists" and their precursors, such as Raymond Queneau (1903–1976). Clearly Barth means to include or even to focus on the Central and South American "magic realists" — a term that came to be applied to some European, British, and American authors as well, including Günter Grass (b. 1927), Jerzy Kosinski (b. 1933), Mark Helprin (b. 1947), and Carter. Indeed, with the rise of magic realism, some neglected American authors of the past, such as Nathanael West with *Miss Lonelyhearts* (1933) seemed newly relevant. But Barth now means to exclude some figures formerly seen as central postmodernists. A postmodernist writer, he argues, "aspires to a fiction more democratic in its appeal than such late-modernist marvels (by my definition and in my judgment) as Beckett's *Stories and Tales for Nothing* or Nabokov's *Pale Fire*."[10] In the same essay, Barth labels Joyce's *Finnegans Wake* an exemplary modernist work, whereas many commentators in the structuralist critical tradition had cast it as the origin of postmodernism.

CONTEMPORARY POSTMODERNISM

In invoking a more "democratic appeal," Barth picks up the strain highlighted by Fiedler and others in the 1960s who saw the new literature within the context of Pop Art, the counterculture, multimedia productions and "happenings," the Beats, and a number of other aspects of subcultures that set themselves in opposition to "official" or "academic" culture. This emotive and demotic postmodernist strain was muffled during the heyday of metafiction in the 1960s and 1970s, which spotlighted formally complex works that often offered the ordinary reader little narrative satisfaction, but it again became dominant in the 1980s. At the same time that formal complexity began to be de-emphasized, the new literature's close relationship with popular or "low" arts and genres was increasingly seen as important and as having political significance. Indeed, many commentators now saw that relationship as postmodernism's defining difference from modernism. Mass culture, which in this interpretation had been the "repressed other" of elitist modernist art, was finally embraced in a postmodernist age.[11]

Changes in the dominant literary theories from the late 1970s to the 1990s may account for much of the shift in critics' construction of postmodernism. While critical theory could be described as "post-structuralist" for that entire span, it underwent a shift from a language-oriented criticism based in Barthes and Derrida that stressed an attack on representation in the earlier part of the period to a power- and discourse-oriented criticism based on Michel Foucault (and to a degree on Mikhail Bakhtin and Jacques Lacan) that was far more interested in marginalized social groups and the way in which even literary forms can solidify the hegemony of dominant social groups (see chap. 1, pp. 28–29).[12] While Foucauldian poststructuralism still welcomed literary experimentation, the American and British critics who utilized it increasingly chose to examine works with a strong narrative line whose main formal interest was that they betrayed some influence of magic realism.

American writers with an ethnic affiliation were a beneficiary of this. Some, such as the Nobel Prize winner Toni Morrison (b. 1931) with major books like *The Bluest Eye* (1970), *Song of Solomon* (1977), and *Beloved* (1987), are such powerful voices they might have thrived in any critical climate; some, like Michael Ondaatje, a Sri Lankan residing in Canada, had already established avant-garde credentials by the 1970s. But the vogue for what we might term "political postmodernism" undoubtedly gave a boost to a number of highly talented writers who might have been overlooked because of the institutionalized racism that still has not been eradicated from the literary-critical profession. These might include Native American writers such as Gerald Vizenor (b. 1934) with *Braveheart* (1990) and Leslie Marmon Silko (b. 1948) with *Ceremony* (1977) and *Almanac of the Dead* (1991); writers of Latin extraction such as Oscar Hijuelos (b. 1951) with *The Mambo Kings Play Songs of Love* (1989) and Gloria Anzaldúa (b. 1942) with her mixed-genre productions; writers of Asian descent like Amy Tan (b. 1952) with *The Joy Luck Club* (1989) and Maxine Hong Kingston (b. 1940) with *The Woman Warrior* (1976). In England, the greatest beneficiaries of the new climate have been writers of Indian origin such as Salman Rushdie (b. 1947), whose acclaimed *Midnight's Children* (1980) prepared no one for the political furor aroused by *The Satanic Verses* (1989). Many of these novels have been termed examples of "historiographic metafiction" and share with most magic realism a serious interest in the exploration of cultural and political history from a perspective other than that of Anglo-American empiricism.

Meanwhile, attempts to define postmodernism in theoretical terms proliferate. The critic Douwe Fokkema argues that "whereas the Modernist aimed at providing a valid, authentic, though strictly personal view of the world in which he lived, the Postmodernist appears to have abandoned the attempt towards a representation of the world that is justified by the convictions and sensibility of an individual."[13] Lyotard argues that the modern condition made its appeal to great narratives or metadiscourses — patterns of thinking that underlie cultural assumptions — while postmodernity is characterized by incredulity toward all such metanarratives.[14] Linda Hutcheon elaborates on the importance of parody in postmodernism, while Fredric Jameson claims that postmodernism is, as his book's subtitle puts it, "the cultural logic of late capitalism." From a Marxist perspective Jameson suggests that we might associate late-nineteenth-century "classical realism" with local or national capitalism; modernism with monopoly capitalism and imperialism; and postmodernism with multinational capital.[15] In an influential formulation, Brian McHale has argued that modernism deals with epistemological concerns, postmodernism with ontological ones, so there is a "shift of dominant from problems of *knowing* to problems of *modes of being.*"[16] In his later work he has tried to modify and refine this formulation.

Common themes among critics of the postmodern are the attack on the unified subject, the attack on representation, the aesthetic importance of chance or of some arbitrary principle in structuring art, and reflexivity or some other experimental formal principle. Occasionally a critic will imply that a work is postmodern if there is a sufficiently radical "breaking of the frame," such as the author appearing within the pages of his or her fiction. Many critics stress postmodernism's breaking down of boundaries between genres (such as between fiction and nonfiction) and between cultural "levels" (such as between "serious" fiction and "genre" fiction). On the model of postmodern architecture, many stress the importance of postmodern "citation" of older forms or even of particular classic works. As the poet Andrei Codrescu (b. 1946) put it, where the modernist Pound had commanded "Make It New," the postmodernist imperative is "Get It Used."[17]

The great majority of critics who choose to write about postmodernism see it as somehow progressive or liberating, although some, such as Gerald Graff, have attacked it from a traditional leftist position.[18] American writers often discussed in this context include Don DeLillo (b. 1936); Walter Abish (b. 1931); Russell Banks (b. 1940); Sandra Cisneros (b. 1954); Paul Auster (b. 1947), with his Beckettian adaptations of the detective story; and Kathy Acker (b. 1948), with her citations and adaptations of passages from classic literature and her use of apparently pornographic passages. British writers often mentioned include John Fowles; A. S. Byatt (b. 1936), especially in *Possession* (1990); Jeanette Winterson (b. 1959); Christine Brooke-Rose (b. 1923); Maggie Gee (b. 1948); Martin Amis (b. 1949); and Julian Barnes (b. 1946), whose *Flaubert's Parrot* is in some ways the paradigmatic poststructuralist novel.

Another perspective on postmodernism relies on Walter Ong's discussions of the "Gutenberg revolution" in which there was a major "paradigm shift" from oral to alphabetic cultures; according to Ong, this involved a fundamental change in patterns of thought and even in the structures of perception. Ong then speculates that a similar change is taking place from alphabetic to cinematic or electronic culture and that postmodernism can be conceptualized as the name for the period of awareness as this second change becomes widespread.[19] The logic of this position would seem to dictate that postmodern art would be cinematic or video or involve some sort of computer interface, though metaphorically some critics extend the term to novels that show a particular awareness of contemporary "electronic culture."[20] Perhaps the purest example of postmodern fiction in this sense is hypertext, in which there is no single linear fictional text but only a series of possibilities produced by a reader's choices. One of the best-known examples of this is Michael Joyce's (b. 1940) *Afternoon*, but there is no doubt that the genre will grow rapidly. Already more conventional novels like Douglas Coupland's (b. 1961) *Generation X* (1991) make some attempts to mimic hypertext graphically.

Postmodernism is still too unwieldy a term to designate anything very specific, and the problem with large general definitions such as Brian McHale's is that they are too abstract to apply very consistently: just how do we tell whether a given novel is more epistemological or more ontological in its concerns? Further, it sometimes appears that modernism has been made a political "whipping boy" for a postmodernism that is somehow conceived as populist, even though few if any postmodern works can claim any sort of mass readership. In the heat of their enthusiasm for postmodernism, critics are apt to blunt modernism's dangerous, experimental edge and begin discussing it as if it were nineteenth-century realism.

Postmodernism may be more a way of reading than a way of writing: virtually any work can be said to have postmodern characteristics if we read it in the right spirit, as a perusal of Sir Walter Scott's *Old Mortality* (1816), with its authorial and fictive prefaces, notes, and afterwords, should demonstrate.[21] What is more, John Barth rightly points out that however we draw our definitions, few writers are consistently any one thing: "Joyce Carol Oates writes all over the aesthetical map. . . . My own novels seem to me to have both modernist and postmodernist attributes; my short story series, *Lost in the Funhouse*, strikes me as mainly late-modernist, though some critics have praised or damned it as conspicuously postmodernist."[22] And finally, just as with modernism, an unresolved difficulty with the concept of the postmodern is that it is used to address, by means of what is most contemporary in criticism, what we find most *contemporary* in writing — and that is bound to change.

NOTES

1. Harry Levin, "What Was Modernism?" *Varieties of Literary Experience,* ed. Stanley Burnshaw (New York: New York UP, 1962) 307–330; Raymond Williams, "When Was Modernism?" *The Politics of Modernism: Against the New Conformists* (London: Verso, 1989) 31–36.

2. For a chronology of uses of the term *postmodern,* see Hans Bertens, *The Idea of the Postmodern: A History* (New York: Routledge, 1995).

3. Boris Ford, ed., *The Modern Age,* vol. 7 of *The Pelican Guide to English Literature,* rev. ed. (Baltimore: Penguin, 1964).

4. George Orwell, "The Rediscovery of Europe" (1942), *The Collected Essays, Journalism, and Letters of George Orwell,* ed. Sonia Orwell and Ian Angus, vol. 2 (New York: Harcourt, 1968) 206.

5. Susan Sontag, "Against Interpretation," *Against Interpretation and Other Essays* (New York: Dell, 1967) 3–14; Ihab Hassan, "The Dismemberment of Orpheus," *American Scholar* 32 (1963): 463–84; Leslie Fiedler, "The New Mutants," *Partisan Review* 32 (1965): 505–25; Frank Kermode, "Modernisms Again: Objects, Jokes, and Art," *Encounter* 26.4 (1966): 65–74. My discussion is indebted to Hans Bertens, *The Idea of the Postmodern: A History* (New York: Routledge, 1995) 23–31.

6. Leslie Fiedler, quoted in Bertens 30.

7. John Barth, "The Literature of Exhaustion," *Atlantic* Aug. 1967: 33.

8. See Raymond Federman, ed., *Surfiction: Fiction Now . . . and Tomorrow* (Chicago: Swallow, 1975), and Patricia Waugh, *Metafiction: The Theory and Practice of Self-Conscious Fiction* (New York: Methuen, 1984).

9. John Barth, "The Literature of Replenishment," *Atlantic* Jan. 1980: 71.

10. Barth, "Literature of Replenishment" 70.

11. Several books that make an assumption like this are Jim Collins, *Uncommon Cultures: Popular Culture and Post-Modernism* (New York: Routledge, 1989); Brian McHale, *Postmodernist Fiction* (New York: Methuen, 1987); and Andreas Huyssen, *After the Great Divide: Modernism, Mass Culture, Postmodernism* (Bloomington: Indiana UP, 1986).

12. This argument is elaborated in Bertens 6–9.

13. Douwe Fokkema, *Literary History, Modernism, and Postmodernism* (Amsterdam: Benjamins, 1984) 40.

14. Jean-François Lyotard, *The Postmodern Condition: A Report on Knowledge,* trans. Geoff Bennington and Brian Massumi (Minneapolis: U of Minnesota P, 1984).

15. Linda Hutcheon, *Poetics of Postmodernism: History, Theory, Fiction* (New York: Routledge, 1988); Fredric Jameson, *Postmodernism, or, the Cul-*

tural Logic of Late Capitalism (Durham: Duke UP, 1991); Jameson, "Cognitive Mapping," *Marxism and the Interpretation of Culture,* eds. Cary Nelson and Lawrence Grossberg (Urbana: U of Illinois P, 1988) 347–360.

16. Brian McHale, *Postmodernist Fiction* (New York: Methuen, 1987) 10.

17. Quoted in David Lehman, "The Questions of Postmodernism," *AWP Chronicle* 27.3: (1994): 4.

18. See Gerald Graff, *Literature Against Itself: Literary Ideas in Modern Society* (Chicago: U of Chicago P, 1979).

19. Walter Ong, *Orality and Literacy: The Technology of the Word* (New York: Methuen, 1982).

20. Robert B. Ray, who is sympathetic to Ong's position, offers a variety of possible beginning dates for postmodernism, from 1836, "when the Parisian *La Presse* became the first commercial daily newspaper," to 1984, "when the U.S. Supreme Court ruled that copyright law did not prohibit home off-the-air video taping." Some intervening dates that he offers are 1954, when more than half of American homes had television, and 1913, when "Marcel Duchamp mounted an upside-down bicycle wheel to a kitchen stool, therefore 'producing' the first 'ready-made' (Duchamp's own term for an everyday object, named, signed, and offered as art)." "Postmodernism," *Encyclopedia of Literature and Criticism,* eds. Martin Coyle et al. (London: Routledge, 1991) 131–150.

21. I am indebted to Rhonda Riley for pointing out this example.

22. Barth, "Literature of Replenishment" 66.

4

The Novel, Race, and Nation

The growth since the mid-1960s of what used to be called "ethnic stud-ies" and the subsequent rise of postcolonial studies is one of the most visible events in the profession of literary criticism. In the United States the largest and most prominent component of minority studies has been devoted to African American literature, art, history, and culture; in some ways it can stand as a model for Latino/Latina studies, Native American studies, Asian American studies, and other such areas.

AFRICAN AMERICAN STUDIES

Although some critical attention had been paid to African American writing during the Harlem Renaissance in the 1920s and also to the work of individual artists, notably Richard Wright and Ralph Ellison, as an area of academic concentration African American studies first came to national attention during the 1960s, as the New Criticism was waning in influ-ence. At the time, it was often seen as part of the general countercultural movement in the United States, with its anti-academic, broadly political, and emotive stance (see chap. 3). The movement, which demanded a re-valuation of African American art in general through the formulation of what became known in the 1960s as the "Black Aesthetic," challenged prevailing critical norms in several ways.

In insisting that art produced by African Americans was fundamentally different from art in the white European tradition, it challenged that tradition's claim to address the whole of the "human condition" in a timeless fashion. In defining a category of art through the persons producing it, the Black Aesthetic could be said to be founded on what was once termed the "intentional fallacy" — and thus to anticipate later critical movements that also thought it important to consider the agents of cultural production.[1] By valuing protest and invoking a variety of Marxism, the Black Aesthetic brought to the fore political questions that the New Criticism saw as irrelevant or secondary. Some commentators have argued that some of the founders of the New Criticism were themselves racist, and they cite lines like Robert Penn Warren's from "Pondy Woods" — "Nigger, your breed ain't metaphysical," a line that spurred the African American poet Sterling Brown (1901–1989) to reply, "Cracker, your breed ain't exegetical."[2] As if to support Brown's bitter quip, the aesthetic of the Black Arts Movement suggested that white readers were not qualified to appreciate black art. As the critic Stephen Henderson wrote in the early 1970s,

> the recognition of Blackness in poetry is a value judgment which . . . notably in matters of meaning that go beyond questions of structure and theme, must rest upon one's immersion in the totality of the Black Experience. It means that the ultimate criteria for critical evaluation must be found in the sources of the creation, that is, in the Black Community itself.[3]

A great deal of the writing celebrated by the Black Arts Movement of the 1960s and 1970s was either poetry, like that of LeRoi Jones (b. 1934; later Amiri Baraka) and Don L. Lee (b. 1942; later Haki R. Madhubuti) or nonfictional autobiographical narrative, like Eldridge Cleaver's (b. 1935) *Soul on Ice* (1967) or like the historical and philosophical writing of African Americans from the earliest slave narratives through the publications and speeches of Booker T. Washington (1856–1915) and the essays of James Baldwin (1924–1987). Despite notable triumphs like Ralph Ellison's *Invisible Man* (1952), the novel was not necessarily a central genre in this tradition. So it was not surprising that when the next wave of African American critics began writing in the late 1970s they should discuss "narrative" rather than "novel." Robert B. Stepto's *From Behind the Veil: A Study of Afro-American Narrative* (1979) represented, among other things, an attempt to integrate Afro-American criticism into the dominant mode of literary criticism of the time, structuralism and semiotics. It was convenient for Stepto's purposes that structuralist criticism had shifted the terms of general theoretical discussion from "novel" to "narrative" already (see chap. 1).

Stepto's assumption is that "if an Afro-American literary tradition exists, it does so not because there is a sizeable chronology of authors and texts, but because those authors and texts collectively seek their own literary forms — their own admixtures of genre — bound historically and linguistically to a shared pre-generic myth." This "pre-generic myth," which Stepto compares to what Northrop Frye calls "canonical stories," is "the quest for freedom and literacy."[4] The two ideas are of course interconnected: for the Enlightenment, to write was to establish oneself as a reasoning being, which was the requirement for being considered human. The genres that concern Stepto include autobiography, fiction, and historiography, but much of his energy is spent on establishing his own terminology for narrative genres — four kinds of slave narrative, which he terms "eclectic," "integrated," "generic," and "authenticating," for example. He finds it more useful to view James Weldon Johnson's *Autobiography of an Ex-Colored Man* (1912) as "an intentionally aborted immersion narrative that revoices both *Up from Slavery* and *The Souls [of Black Folk]*," Richard Wright's *Black Boy* as a narrative of ascent, and Ellison's *Invisible Man* as "a narrative of hibernation." Indeed, Stepto prefers "to use terms such as 'epiloging text' and 'narrative' instead of 'modern text' and 'novel.' "[5] Perhaps more influential than his taxonomies and terms has been Stepto's tracing of each text's "revoicing" of earlier texts, which he sometimes figures as "call and response," from the structure of African American religious services.

Also in 1979 Stepto and Dexter Fisher edited a collection of essays and materials entitled *Afro-American Literature: The Reconstruction of Instruction*, whose theme was the necessity of reconceiving the teaching of Afro-American literature on a more rigorous basis, meaning in a way rooted in the study of literature and language. One of the most prominent contributors to the collection was Henry Louis Gates, Jr., then Stepto's colleague at Yale. Both Gates and Stepto emphasized a text-based criticism[6] and were attacked at some length for this emphasis by Houston Baker, a distinguished critic who had begun by identifying himself with critics of the Black Aesthetic and has gradually elaborated a complex critical position based on the spoken word.[7] In fact, Stepto and Fisher's volume included several essays with a multidisciplinary emphasis, and this, rather than a strictly language-oriented criticism, was to be the major direction of African American criticism in the 1980s. Gates in particular articulated a complex and flexible approach in *The Signifying Monkey* (1988).

Gates takes the "signifying monkey," his term for an African trickster figure well known in folklore, as his "figure-of-figures," the "trope in which are encoded several other peculiarly black rhetorical tropes."[8] "Signifying," Gates's key concept, has a special meaning in jazz but more generally for Gates means *repetition with revision*; in the black tradition this includes "marking, loud-talking, testifying, calling (of one's name), sounding, rapping, playing the dozens, and so on."[9] For Gates, it is close to a principle of linguistic *play*, and so in one way approximates a principle that linguistically oriented poststructuralist critics find most significant in literature. Gates is not simply linguistic in his interest, though, and often invokes Foucault's term *discourse* in its broadest sense. But Mikhail Bakhtin is the literary critic upon whom Gates relies most, especially in his notion of "double-voiced discourse" (see chap. 1). For Bakhtin, double-voicedness can include anything from writing directed toward a particular audience, anticipating its response, to pastiche and full-blown parody. Bakhtin is also useful for Gates because his concept of language is based in oral speech and includes ideology, allowing Gates to deal with the political issues that seem inseparable from African American studies.

A similar idea of double-voicedness seems to be evoked in some of Houston Baker's later writings. In *Modernism and the Harlem Renaissance* (1987), for example, he makes a clear distinction between African American modernism, as embodied in the Harlem Renaissance, and Anglo-European modernism, a movement he sees as alien to his people. But he invokes the minstrel mask, a metaphor that suggests that African American art often both impersonates a white construction of itself and playfully undermines that construction from within.[10] Elsewhere, Baker uses the blues as his dominant metaphor, suggesting tradition, improvisation, vernacular roots, and protest; and he builds some critical bridges to the political wing of postmodernism, notably the work of Foucault and Fredric Jameson.[11] More recently, Baker has focused on African American women's writing, in an attempt to establish its "poetic," while an increasing number of significant discussions by African American women such as Barbara Christian, Hazel Carby, and bell hooks have explored the topic from within.[12]

How does African American studies reconfigure the concept of the novel that preceded it? In the first place, it is apparent that the genre is far less "natural" an analytic category than it appears in the Anglo-American tradition. Many of the novel's basic narratives, such as the rise within society or the search for identity during youth, look entirely different for African Americans. Most critics have found it valuable to examine African American novels from a multidisciplinary stance, because (for example) the role of folklore in novels by Zora Neale Hurston is far more important than in novels by her American contemporary John Dos Passos, or because African myth in Toni Morrison's *Song of Solomon* lends a structuring presence. Indeed, the recent "return to history" of the critical community looks odd from the perspective of African American studies, where history was always of fundamental importance.

Aside from these formal and generic considerations, African American studies is like many contemporary critical approaches, from the feminist through the Marxist, in putting into question the white American and Eurocentric canon as a whole, even as it rereads each individual work from that canon. Toni Morrison's recent study of American literature, *Playing in the Dark* (1992), suggests that blackness is the great unspoken subject of most white American literature, a theme and image that shapes literature even as it is repressed within it.[13] Whatever the merits of Morrison's readings, there can be no doubt that every work of literature written by white Americans is changed if we read it with some awareness of the cultural context of black Americans. As Houston Baker points out, Lionel Trilling's assertion that modernism poses fundamental and personal questions to the reader depends on the particular reader: "It is difficult . . . for an Afro-American student of literature like me — one unconceived in the philosophies of Anglo-American, British, and Irish moderns — to find intimacy either in the moderns' hostility to *civilization* or in their fawning reliance on an array of images and assumptions bequeathed by a *civilization* that . . . is exclusively Western, preeminently bourgeois, and optically white."[14] (Here Baker may be recalling Mahatma Gandhi's famous reply to reporters who asked him, "What do you think of Western civilization, Mr. Gandhi?" "I think," he responded, "that it would be a good idea.")

POSTCOLONIAL STUDIES

Since the rise of what has come to be called postcolonial studies — sometimes written "(post)-colonial," to indicate graphically that colonization is not a simple event with a simple ending — African American studies to some extent has been swept up in its larger context. This is not a new issue: during the 1960s, for instance, there were frequent calls for the culture of American blacks to be examined against a broader background. The Negritude movement centering in northern Africa and much of the Caribbean during the 1960s, for instance, had obvious relevance to the Black Aesthetic, as it attempted to define a black culture, philosophy, and even a time and space different from that of the European tradition. The more recent rise of studies of other minority cultures has been another factor, demonstrating that some of the patterns, themes, and principles that have emerged regarding the culture of American blacks might have relevance to the situation of West Indians in London or even that of Chicanos and Chicanas in Los Angeles *barrios*.

From the perspective of the novel, perhaps the central question posed by colonial and postcolonial studies is the one prompted by its name: does the fact of the colonial experience constitute the major determining factor in any examination of literature from former or present colonies? A powerful positive argument is posed by the neo-Marxist critic Fredric Jameson in an article entitled "Third-World Literature in the Era of Multinational Capitalism." Jameson begins by pointing out that the difficulty in expanding the canon by adding "non-canonical forms of literature such as that of the third world" is that we often try to apply traditional European standards to them and of course often find the new candidates lacking.[15] Jameson's solution is to propose that we interpret (and thus by implication value) third world novels differently. He suggests that Western novels show a clear division between the realms of the social and the political on the one hand and the world of private existence on the other. Jameson then proposes that the relation between these worlds is radically different in the postcolonial novel, and that in it *"the story of the private individual destiny is always an allegory of the embattled situation of the public third-world culture and society."*[16]

Jameson himself points out a danger of his position — that *"any articulation of radical difference — that of gender, incidentally, fully as much as that of culture — is susceptible to appropriation by that strategy of otherness which Edward Said, in the context of the Middle East, called 'orientalism.'"*[17] Said in his hugely influential book *Orientalism* (1978) argued that the West has always projected its own universal "Other" onto the variety of cultures it calls the Orient, and the logic of this process turns the "oriental" into something objectified, unknowable, feminized, dehistoricized, ripe for colonization, and so forth.[18] As Jameson realizes, this is a danger whether one consciously intends praise of the "other" or not — Conrad's praise for several qualities of the "natives" in *Heart of Darkness* certainly does not make them independent "subjects" comparable to the European males in his novel. But Jameson sees no way for the Western intellectual to avoid such problems.

An equally widely read response to his essay appeared several issues later, entitled "Jameson's Rhetoric of Otherness and the 'National Allegory.'" In it Aijaz Ahmad rejects nearly all of Jameson's presuppositions.

First, he argues "that there is no such thing as a 'third-world literature' which can be constructed as an internally coherent object of theoretical knowledge," and therefore there is no possibility of "a theory of cognitive aesthetics for third-world literature."[19] Ahmad points out that opposing the "first world" of Europe and America to the "second world" of the (former) socialist bloc and both of these to the "underdeveloped" or "developing" nations is useless because of the huge variety of cultures and their relationships to nationhood or capitalism.

Ahmad makes two important points along the way that challenge Jameson's approach to postcoloniality. First, by tracing the development of the novel in Urdu, he gives the reader a sense that Jameson's theory of national allegory does no justice to its social and literary complexity: Ahmad's implication is that cultures in the "third world" are so different from one another that it is meaningless to group them. His second point is that if we consider the contexts of feminism and of black literature, we can see that "there is right here, within the belly of the first world's global postmodernism, a veritable third world, perhaps two or three of them."[20] The third world has no monopoly on allegory, he indicates — novels by members of oppressed minorities (such as Ellison's *Invisible Man*) naturally accrue more than personal significance. Overall, Ahmad seems to be suggesting that whereas Marxism supplies conceptual tools that have some universal bearing, the colonial and postcolonial situation, at least as it is currently theorized, does not do so.

Some of these problems can be found within the very term *postcolonial*, as several commentators have pointed out. Ella Shohut notes that the term has come into prominence as the term *third world* has faded and suggests that the enthusiasm for postcolonial studies in a rather conservative academy is evidence that it is no longer conceived as dangerous or activist. In this regard, Shohut argues, "the 'post-colonial' implies both going beyond anti-colonial nationalist theory as well as a movement beyond a specific point in history, that of colonialism and Third World nationalist struggles."[21] The problem with this is, naturally, that some form of colonialism is still very much in force in most of the less-developed areas of the world. The term also suggests, by similarity, ties to poststructuralist criticism, not all of whose varieties are politically activist.

Setting aside for the moment the issue of terminology, the central question here for our purposes is whether there is a pattern imposed on the postcolonial novel, or at least an interpretive direction, that has aesthetic significance. As was discussed in chapter 1, particularly coherent schools of interpretation tend to impose their own patterns of meaning on texts — or allow them readily to be identified in the texts and announced as their "real meaning." Many of the critics writing in postcolonialism today have a background in deconstructive criticism, which brands the Western philosophical tradition as "phallogocentric" — a way of yoking together the rule of phallic authority and logocentrism, a fetish with the spoken word as an embodiment of that presence and authority. The tendency is for deconstructionist critics to see imperialism as a large and dangerous example of this philosophical error and to interpret both the discourse of colonialism and writings by the colonized in this ultimate perspective.

The majority of critics working in the postcolonial field today have Marxist sympathies — and after all it was Lenin's book *Imperialism, the Highest Stage of Capitalism* (1916) that put colonialism firmly into the Marxist matrix. Gayatri Chakravorty Spivak's essay "Can the Subaltern Speak?" borrows from the Western Marxist Antonio Gramsci the term *subaltern* — which both means "a person of inferior rank" and has particular reference to military rank in colonial India.[22] But Spivak's own position embodies many of the conflicts that postcolonial studies holds in uneasy tension: she is a woman from India who is very highly placed in the Anglo-American critical establishment; she made her reputation as a deconstructionist and is also regarded as a feminist and to some serious degree a Marxist, while some of her work shows an interest in psychoanalysis. A collection of interviews with her has been published under the title *The Post-Colonial Critic* (1990), while she has recently attacked postcolonialism as "just totally bogus."[23]

Despite such potential and real contradictions, the field has considerable internal coherence. The authors of the first important survey of postcolonial theory and practice — which has the catchy title *The Empire Writes Back* (1989) — point out that a number of themes emerge from a study of literatures as disparate as those of New Zealand *pakeha* (white settlers), Indians, and Kenyans. Among these are the struggle toward independence in the individual and in the community, the dominance of a foreign culture on indigenous life, and even specific motifs such as the construction or demolition of a house or the journey taken by a European interloper with a native guide. Critics have also pointed to the distinctive use of allegory (such as Jameson suggests), a particular kind of irony, and magic realism.[24] Even postmodernism itself has been discussed as the "natural" mode of postcolonial writing, and its current dominance has been portrayed as an implicit confession on the part of Western culture that it has reached a point of exhaustion and must be revived by previously marginalized artists.[25] But not all interpretations of postcoloniality are so positive. V. S. Naipaul (b. 1932), in what more sanguine critics have since termed the "Naipaul fallacy," has implied that colonization is such

an overwhelming cultural experience that it leaves the colonized perma-
nently disabled, attempting to mimic the metropolitan culture that has
swamped them where they stand on the periphery.[26]

One of the questions with which postcolonial study wrestles is whether
there are meaningful similarities in the experiences of colonial settlers of
what has been called the "white diaspora" of the nineteenth century —
Canadians, Australians, South Africans, and New Zealanders, for example — and those of the "black diaspora." In each of the former cases,
the white colonizers are under the hegemony of the colonizing country
and in turn exert hegemony over the indigenes. The classic case of this is,
of course, the United States, where a former colony later becomes a major imperial power and includes its own "colonized" minorities — perhaps the least numerous of whom are descendants of the original
inhabitants. A great deal of literary criticism has of course been devoted
to the idea of "American exceptionalism" — the premise that American
experience is best understood through its basic difference from that of
Europeans — and the concomitant idea that "American literature" has a
characteristic form, such as the romance, or theme, such as the possession of a frontier or the idea of a New Eden that is pastoral rather than
urban.[27]

The United States is clearly an unusual case; but so is Ireland, for instance, which for many years was an example of imperialist (and even
racist) domination of white men over other whites. Yet Ireland has produced many "canonical" literary figures — Yeats, Joyce, Shaw, Wilde —
all of whom saw themselves in different ways as Irish or as British or as
both. Recently these figures have begun to be examined from a postcolonial
perspective — although, of course, Northern Ireland is still part of the
British Empire.[28] Similarly, Katherine Mansfield is now occasionally read
not only as a modernist, but as a *pakeha* (white) writer of New Zealand,
while thoroughly "assimilated" writers like V. S. Naipaul (b. 1932) of
Trinidad and R. K. Narayan (b. 1906) of India are being reread from a
postcolonial perspective.

The richest legacy of postcolonialism is, of course, its opening of the
canon to writers in the English language — but not necessarily in the
Anglo-American literary tradition. Writers who do not fit into the traditional curriculum, with its choice of "American" (meaning United States)
or "British" (meaning British Isles, including Ireland) literature might
include Janet Frame (b. 1924) and Frank Sargeson (b. 1903) of New
Zealand; Sinclair Ross (b. 1908), Margaret Laurence (1926–1987),
Robertson Davies (1913–1996), Alice Munro (b. 1931), and Margaret
Atwood (b. 1939) of Canada; Wilson Harris (b. 1921), George Lamming

(b. 1927), Merle Hodge (b. 1944), and Jamaica Kincaid (b. 1949) of the
Caribbean; Shashi Tharoor (b. 1956), Rohinton Mistry (b. 1952), and
Amitav Ghosh (b. 1956) of India; and Wole Soyinka (b. 1934), Chinua
Achebe (b. 1930), Ngugi wa Thiong'o (b. 1938), Kofi Awoonor (b. 1935),
Ayi Kwei Armah (b. 1939), Alex LaGuma (1925–1985), Bessie Head (b.
1937), Ama Ata Aidoo (b. 1942), and Buchi Emecheta (b. 1944) of vari-
ous African nations.

Does an overwhelming experience of group identity such as colonization outweigh the experience of racial identity? Some of the essays in
Henry Louis Gates, Jr.'s collection *"Race," Writing, and Difference* (1986)
address this issue. Does it outweigh the experience of gender identification? Both Spivak and Chandra Mohanty have negotiated the conflicting
claims of feminism and postcoloniality, even as Jean Rhys (1890–1979),
Doris Lessing (b. 1919), Toni Morrison (b. 1931), Paule Marshall (b. 1929),
and Margaret Atwood (b. 1939) have drawn an analogy between male-
female relationships and those of the imperial power and the colony. Which
is more fundamental in the "construction of the subject"? How does imperial capitalism, or for that matter multinational capitalism, fit into the
equation? The European founding fathers of modernity — Marx, Freud,
and Darwin — have all been marshaled and updated in an effort to grapple
with this kind of problem.

Another current issue in postcolonial studies is that of *hybridity* or
syncretism, two terms pointing to the typically mixed cultural lineage of
postcolonial writers. The Guyanese novelist and critic Wilson Harris has
stressed the potentially liberating aspect of this situation, in which "hybridity in the present is constantly struggling to free itself from a past
which stressed ancestry, and which valued the 'pure' over its threatening
opposite, the 'composite.'"[29] After all, postcolonial novels are characteris-
tically hybrid, multicultural productions, showing the influence of many
genres, only some of which belong to the European cultural tradition.
Their authors, too, have multiple national affiliations, as the cases of Mario
Vargas Llosa (b. 1936), Bharati Mukherjee (b. 1940), Carlos Fuentes (b.
1928), Derek Walcott (b. 1930), Isabel Allende (b. 1942), and Salman
Rushdie (b. 1947) demonstrate. Rushdie, for instance, is a Bombay-born
Muslim who was trained at Cambridge and lived in London, attached to a
family that was relocated to Pakistan in the mid-1970s. Carlos Fuentes (b.
1928), known as a Mexican novelist, was born in Panama, raised mostly in
the United States, and is closely linked to France. Clearly these writers
are cosmopolitan, international figures, and their writing has redefined
the contemporary novel. But they have also been critiqued from the left
as holding themselves aloof from the people they represent, writing work

that discusses colonialism but not from an activist perspective. Further, it has been argued that their writing is so celebrated in North American literature departments precisely because it is fundamentally *familiar*; the novels that they write are, after all, an imported genre in most of the third world.[30]

Perhaps the most useful contemporary thinker for postcolonial studies, because of his linkage of power, knowledge, and language, is Michel Foucault (whose work stands behind much of Said's work on Orientalism). But Foucault is notoriously ambiguous about hope for the future, and it is unclear whether within his system the resistance that is almost automatically generated by the writings of the colonized will have an important effect on the "discourse of colonialism." On a literal level, Ngugi wa Thiong'o's call for a return to writing in precolonial languages may be the logical conclusion of a Foucaultian analysis.[31] What are the political possibilities of novels of protest against colonization by the colonizers, such as Alan Paton's (b. 1903) *Cry, the Beloved Country* (1948) or E. M. Forster's *Passage to India* (1924)? What about the works of white South Africans such as Nadine Gordimer (b. 1923) and J. M. Coetzee (b. 1940)? Are their explicitly progressive politics debased by the novel form itself and by the necessary "othering" that European writing inflicts on the non-European? At the simplest level, is the novel itself an agent of colonization? To a Eurocentric humanist, this proposition would seem both horrifying and silly; but then, poststructuralist critics are not humanists. And this is the sort of issue that will continue to be debated in postcolonial studies.

NOTES

1. W. K. Wimsatt and Monroe C. Beardsley, "The Intentional Fallacy" (1946), *The Verbal Icon: Studies in the Meaning of Poetry* (Lexington: U of Kentucky P, 1954).

2. Cited in Henry Louis Gates, Jr., "Writing 'Race' and the Difference It Makes," *"Race," Writing, and Difference* (Chicago: U of Chicago P, 1986) 4.

3. Stephen Henderson, "The Forms of Things Unknown," *Understanding the New Black Poetry, Black Speech, and Black Music as Poetic References* (New York: Morrow, 1973), quoted in Houston A. Baker, Jr., *Blues, Ideology, and Afro-American Literature: A Vernacular Theory* (Chicago: U of Chicago P, 1984) 79.

4. Robert B. Stepto, "Preface to the First Edition," *From Behind the Veil: A Study of Afro-American Narrative*, 2nd ed. (Urbana: U of Illinois P, 1991) xv–xvi.

5. Stepto, xvi, xviii.

6. Robert B. Stepto, "Teaching Afro-American Literature: Survey or Tradition," *Afro-American Literature: The Reconstruction of Instruction,* ed. Dexter Fisher and Robert B. Stepto (New York: MLA, 1979) 8–24; Henry Louis Gates, Jr., "Preface to Blackness: Text and Pretext," *Afro-American Literature* 44–70.

7. Baker 87–112.

8. Henry Louis Gates, Jr., *The Signifying Monkey: A Theory of African-American Literary Criticism* (New York: Oxford UP, 1988) xxi.

9. Gates, *Signifying* 52.

10. Houston A. Baker, Jr., *Modernism and the Harlem Renaissance* (Chicago: U of Chicago P, 1987) 17. Note that some critics of Anglo-European modernism in fact have attempted to link the minstrel show metaphor with the development of modernism itself, thus reattaching the two traditions and showing a debt of the dominant tradition to the minority one. See Michael North, *The Dialect of Modernism: Race, Language, and Twentieth-Century Literature* (New York: Oxford UP, 1994).

11. Baker.

12. Houston A. Baker, Jr., *Workings of the Spirit: The Poetics of Afro-American Women's Writing* (Chicago: U of Chicago P, 1990); Barbara Christian, *Black Women Novelists: The Development of a Tradition, 1892–1976* (Westport: Greenwood, 1980); Hazel Carby, *Reconstructing Womanhood: The Emergence of the Afro-American Woman Novelist* (New York: Oxford UP, 1987); bell hooks, *Ain't I a Woman: Black Women and Feminism* (Boston: South End, 1981).

13. Toni Morrison, *Playing in the Dark: Whiteness and the Literary Imagination* (Cambridge: Harvard UP, 1992).

14. Baker, *Modernism* 6.

15. Fredric Jameson, "Third-World Literature in the Era of Multinational Capitalism," *Social Text* 15 (Fall 1986): 65.

16. Jameson 69; Jameson's emphasis.

17. Jameson 77.

18. Edward W. Said, *Orientalism* (New York: Random, 1978).

19. Aijaz Ahmad, "Jameson's Rhetoric of Otherness and the 'National Allegory,'" *Social Text* 17 (Fall 1987): 9.

20. Ahmad 24–25.

21. Ella Shohut, "Notes on the 'Post-Colonial,'" *Social Text* 31/32 (1994): 101.

22. Gayatri Chakravorty Spivak, "Can the Subaltern Speak?" *Colonial Discourse and Post-Colonial Theory: A Reader,* ed. Patrick Williams and Laura Chrisman (New York: Columbia UP, 1994) 66–111.

23. Quoted in "Colonial Discourse and Post-Colonial Theory: An Introduction," *Colonial Discourse* 5–6.

24. Bill Ashcroft, Gareth Griffiths, and Helen Tiffin, *The Empire Writes Back: Theory and Practice in Post-Colonial Literatures* (London: Routledge, 1989) 27–28.

25. "Postmodernism can best be defined as European culture's aware-ness that it is no longer the unquestioned and dominant centre of the world." Robert Young, *White Mythologies: Writing History and the West* (London: Routledge, 1990) 19.

26. Young 88–91. See V. S. Naipaul, *The Mimic Men* (New York: Macmillan, 1967).

27. The "romance" idea was fully articulated in Richard V. Chase, *The American Novel and Its Tradition* (Garden City: Doubleday, 1957). The "fron-tier thesis" was put forth by the historian Frederick Jackson Turner and adapted for literary criticism in Edwin Fussell, *Frontier: American Literature and the American West* (Princeton: Princeton UP, 1965). Leo Marx elaborated the pastoral thesis in *The Machine in the Garden: The Technology and the Pasto-ral Idea in America* (New York: Oxford UP, 1964).

28. See, for instance, David Lloyd, *Anomalous States: Irish Writing and the Post-Colonial Movement* (Durham: Duke UP, 1993), and Vincent Cheng, *Joyce, Race, and Empire* (Cambridge: Cambridge UP, 1995).

29. Ashcroft et al. 35–36.

30. See, for example, Tim Brennan, "Cosmopolitans and Celebrities," *Race and Class* 31.1 (1989): 1–19.

31. Ngugi wa Thiong'o, *Decolonising the Mind: The Politics of Language in African Literature* (London: Currey, 1986).

5

Gender Criticism

Writing in 1981, the critic Wayne Booth suggested that the two recent developments in criticism that had forced him to rethink his position, in a "somewhat surprised surrender to voices previously alien to me," were the work of Bakhtin and feminist criticism.[1] Most critics would simply name feminism, which is not so much an interpretive school like others as it is a revision of the grounds of interpretation themselves. Perhaps Booth's admission here can stand for the belated and reluctant admission by the predominantly white, male academy that at least one major factor in the evaluation of literature had been programmatically ignored. Feminism is, of course, not merely a literary approach but a worldwide social movement and philosophy, or group of philosophies. It has altered not only the accepted canon of literary works we study and the kinds of interpretation we bring to bear on them, but the very language we all speak and the laws and customs that formalize our cultural consensus. The history of feminism broadly conceived is as old as patriarchy and can be traced at least to the ancient Greeks. But modern feminist literary criticism is more directly indebted to the work of feminist writers of the early twentieth century. Most significant for our conception of the novel is Virginia Woolf's work, in particular her long essay *A Room of One's Own* (1929).

In that book and elsewhere in her writing, Woolf can be said to combine materialist and idealist approaches to the question of women's experience. Her starting point is the assumption that in order to become a writer a modern woman needs a "room of her own" and a reasonable

93

independent income. Woolf imagines the disaster that would have be-
fallen a fictional sister of Shakespeare who attempted to support herself
as a playwright and traces the abiding prejudices against women in British and European culture that have made it difficult for them to be taken
seriously as writers — or, because they have internalized some of these
prejudices, to take themselves seriously as artists. She suggests that
women's experience, which has tended to be domestic and interpersonal,
focused on daily things, is a potentially valuable field for the novel.

Woolf states that there is an egocentric "man's sentence" dominant in
the novel that is unsuited to women's use, and thus she implies a "woman's
sentence" natural to women writers — a notion that has led to charges
that Woolf is "essentialist" about women, ascribing some sort of fixed,
eternal identity to them. Woolf nowhere describes the woman's sentence,
but her own distinctive sentences — long, associative, lyrical, full of modi-
fiers and sudden swerves of meaning — might qualify. Finally, Woolf affirms that the writer must necessarily be imaginatively *androgynous*, an
idea Samuel Taylor Coleridge had developed in the early nineteenth century. Questions first clearly articulated by Woolf — whether there is a
recognizable woman's "voice" in literature, whether there is a "natural
subject" for women writers, to what extent personal experience and political ideology are intertwined — are still vigorously debated.

ANGLO-AMERICAN FEMINISM

Feminism first affected literary criticism profoundly in America in the
late 1960s and 1970s. Feminists usually call this a period of rediscovery,
recovery, and reevaluation of writing by women on the one hand and, on
the other, a period of reinterpretation of literature by men reflecting upon
women. The most famous example of the first category is Elaine Showalter's *A Literature of Their Own* (1977), while Ellen Moers in *Literary
Women: The Great Writers* (1976) and Patricia Meyer Spacks in *The Female Imagination* (1975) offer their own approaches to a tradition of
women's writing. The most significant book of the second category, with
an effect felt far beyond the academy, is Kate Millett's *Sexual Politics*
(1970). After two sections concentrating on ideology and history from a
feminist perspective — to explain the whole notion of sexual politics to a
general readership — Millett focuses on prestigious male writers, notably D. H. Lawrence, Henry Miller, and Norman Mailer, who have what
she sees as a pronounced misogynist streak in their work.

In a way, Millett applies Victorian humanistic standards of wholeness and health and shows how misogyny cripples these writers' visions of humanity. She also demonstrates that shockingly misogynist premises can be fundamental to the writing of these men without affecting their reputations: the culture is simply blind to it, just as it had often been blind to institutionalized racism inside or outside of literature. If it took the Black Aesthetic of the 1960s to make white readers realize that there was racism even in a "liberal" classic like *Adventures of Huckleberry Finn*, it took the modern feminist movement to show the misogyny in "liberating" writers like Mailer — or at least to show that it was significant. Millett's practice of liberally quoting passages out of context was criticized, as was her easy identification between the ideas of a character and those of the author, but no doubt her powerful polemical approach contributed to the popular success of her book. And few critics could deny that, if one accepted her premises, she had thoroughly proved her point.

Elaine Showalter, like many other academics during this "heroic phase of feminist criticism,"[2] concentrated on examining the succession of women writers, especially novelists, in Britain, for the most part in the nineteenth century. Unlike Ellen Moers and Patricia Spacks,[3] Showalter does not affirm an actual *tradition* of women writers, but she does present them as a "literary subculture"[4] and in the process unearths many details of the late-nineteenth-century feminist movement. Writers following World War I such as Dorothy Richardson and Virginia Woolf might have been consciously developing a "female aesthetic," but Showalter sees their inwardness and self-involvement as a retreat for women writers.

Meanwhile, other early feminists were redirecting attention to women novelists that the academy already acknowledged to be of the first rank — such as Jane Austen and George Eliot — and questioning the ranking allotted to writers such as Charlotte Brontë (whose *Villette* [1853] has been a feminist favorite ever since Millett's discussion of it), Elizabeth Gaskell (1810–1865), Maria Edgeworth (1768–1849), Elizabeth Inchbald (1753–1821), and Fanny Burney (1752–1840). Fresh attention was paid even to writers whom the New Criticism had relegated to the outer darkness of popular literature, such as Harriet Beecher Stowe, author of *Uncle Tom's Cabin* (1852). Some writers, such as the American Charlotte Perkins Gilman (1860–1935) with her now-famous story "The Yellow Wallpaper" (1892), were rescued from virtually total neglect. Kate Chopin's (1851–1904) *The Awakening* (1899) found its way onto literary syllabi, while novels by Edith Wharton and Willa Cather were more regularly found there as well.

By and large, the rescue of these authors involved a rereading as well. For those writers who did not deliberately espouse a feminist viewpoint, the rereading often included the discovery of a feminist subtext; indeed, the canonical women writers could also be "rescued" in this way. Perhaps the most influential such project was Sandra Gilbert and Susan Gubar's massive study of nineteenth-century British women novelists, *The Madwoman in the Attic* (1979). Gilbert and Gubar posit a female "anxiety of influence" and a repressed feminism among most significant women writers and try to show this in extended readings of Jane Austen, Mary Shelley, Emily and Charlotte Brontë, and George Eliot. They argue that novels by women are "palimpsests," examples of writing in multiple layers, in which a text of feminist protest is often concealed by a text of accommodation to patriarchy.

Their title, the fundamental image of the book, refers to Rochester's first wife in *Jane Eyre*, and their argument is that she is the repressed, raging other self of the relatively docile Jane. A different but related idea had already been implied by the modernist novelist Jean Rhys — herself rediscovered by feminists — who in *Wide Sargasso Sea* (1966) wrote a "prequel" to *Jane Eyre* that begins in Dominica and Jamaica in the 1830s and is narrated mostly from the point of view of the "madwoman," Antoinette Cosway. Gilbert and Gubar have also attempted a rereading and reshaping of the twentieth-century canon, in their multivolume work *No Man's Land: The Place of the Woman Writer in the Twentieth Century*.[5] Bonnie Kime Scott, in an explicit attempt to establish an alternative twentieth-century canon, has compiled an anthology of work by women who could be called "modernist" but who are usually omitted from modernist syllabi. Among the expected names (Djuna Barnes, Katherine Mansfield, Gertrude Stein, Dorothy Richardson) are lesser-known ones such as Nancy Cunard (1896–1965), Nella Larsen, Rose Macaulay (1881–1958), and Antonia White (b. 1899). Scott has also included passages from the famous male modernists, many of which suggest a consensus of male modernist misogyny.[6]

While one stream of the early feminist movement in literary criticism was exploring the idea of a tradition of woman writers and questioning the positioning of both women as subjects and women writers within the patriarchal canon, another stream was attempting to respond to the questions Woolf had raised: Is there a woman's sentence, style, or form? And is there a woman's subject matter? Or, given the interdependency of form and content, is there some characteristic orientation involving both, either historical or "natural," that might be assigned to women? Annis Pratt, for example, has argued that there is a coherent body of novels by women

spanning three centuries with "archetypal patterns" distinct from u.
male writers. In *Archetypal Patterns in Women's Fiction* (1981), she examines novels of initiation into adulthood (the female Bildungsroman);
novels of entry into marriage and social involvement ("novels of enclo-
sure"); novels of the quest for sexuality ("novels of Eros"); and novels of
the quest for personal transformation ("novels of rebirth"). At each phase,
she claims, "the orderly pattern of development is disrupted by social
norms dictating powerlessness for women."[7]

Avoiding this archetypal approach, Rachel Blau DuPlessis in *Writing
beyond the Ending* (1985) still finds a group of characteristic "narrative
strategies" used by women novelists, mostly in order to "delegitimate"
conventional plots such as the romance that were ideologically threatening or uncomfortable for woman writers. For example, in twentieth-century romances by women, the heroine often goes off with a couple instead
of marrying a suitor.[8] A very different approach is represented by Judith
Kegan Gardner, who draws on Nancy Chodorow's feminist revision of
Freud in *The Reproduction of Mothering* (1978). Gardner finds a reflec-
tion of the difference between male and female personality structures in
women's writing, suggesting first that "the heroine is her author's daugh-
ter," with all the implications that that metaphor entails, and second that
for women "the self is defined through social relationships; issues of fu-
sion and merger of the self with others are significant, and ego and body
boundaries remain flexible."[9] Effects like these might be found in a novel's
stylistic and narrative strategies, in its characterization, or even in its plot.

FRENCH FEMINISM

Feminist criticism in the past fifteen years or so has experienced a
number of encounters that have vastly altered its shape. The first of these
was with the Continental critical schools, especially deconstruction (see
p. 28), which challenged many of the pragmatic assumptions about what
constitutes reality on which early feminism had been built. Because of its
stress on linguistic "free play" and its attack on the unified, speaking personal self or "subject" — and thus on most of the bases of Western humanism — Jacques Derrida's deconstruction seemed to undermine the
position of protest assumed by feminist critics. Other poststructuralist
critics, notably Jacques Lacan and Michel Foucault, argued that even
sexual identity was at least partly determined through social discourse
and like other aspects of identity was highly problematic. Somewhat un-
fairly, some of the early feminist literary-critical work in America was

attacked as philosophically naive. As Janet Todd puts it, "A massive inferi-
ority complex was immediately delivered to women who still considered
it radical to discover unpublished stories by Kate Chopin or to suggest
that Sylvia Plath's poems should be in the canon."[10]

A second challenge was the arrival of "French feminism" in translation. A group of Continental literary theoreticians, of whom the most famous were Luce Irigaray, Hélène Cixous, and Julia Kristeva, variously
combined poststructuralist thought with their own variety of feminism —
intellectually radical, but from the pragmatic Anglo-American point of
view only dubiously political. They theorized a women's "space" that pre-
exists the Oedipal trauma and the initiation into the public realm of linguistic patriarchy that Lacan terms the "symbolic." Cixous postulated that
écriture féminine, female or feminine writing, could disrupt the very bases
of patriarchal "logos" with its binary oppositions that underlie all the systems of cultural and political repression — the linguistic drive to speak in
oppositions like white/black, male/female, in which similarities are sup-
pressed and one term is tacitly preferred over the other. *Écriture féminine*
is similar to what Irigaray terms *le parler femme* (sometimes translated
"womanspeak") and its "space" resembles what Kristeva terms "the
semiotic." This concept connected French feminism with stylistically experimental, avant-garde writing such as that practiced by Cixous or by
Gertrude Stein — or, for that matter, by James Joyce, whose *Finnegans
Wake* would seem to fit the description of *écriture féminine*. It also suggested that from the French perspective Anglo-American feminism, working within the system of discourse set up by patriarchy, had no hope of
escaping patriarchy's reach. Yet "French feminism" had its own philosophical dangers. Cixous writing as woman — even if she insisted that
biological sex was irrelevant — suggested to some readers that she was
embracing notions of the essential Mother, the body, nurturance, sexuality, alogical associative processes, and other "archetypal" ideas of womanhood that were endorsed by patriarchy at its most repressive.

During the 1980s academic feminism more or less assimilated Continental theory. Alice Jardine, Toril Moi, and Shari Benstock all had a hand
in building bridges between European and Anglo-American feminist literary discourse.[11] But it can be argued that as it did so it lost its original
focus and political impetus. An important book by Nancy Armstrong,
Desire and Domestic Fiction (1987), illustrates this: Armstrong, following
Foucault, says that her aim is "to show how the discourse of sexuality is
implicated in shaping the novel, and to show as well how domestic fiction
helped to produce a subject who understood herself in the psychological
terms that had shaped fiction." Quite specifically, she states that she is *not*

"constructing a woman's history from the viewpoint of an oppressed or silent minority."[12]

Some would argue that to that extent her work, though clearly influenced by feminism, is dubiously feminist. Others would claim that Armstrong is merely pursuing a different feminist agenda. In any case, it is an example of the emerging field of gender studies. Armstrong argues that as the middle class displaced the upper classes in the nineteenth century, gender differences came to subordinate all other social differences, and the novel was an important means by which this distinction was articulated. So one implication of her work — shared by virtually all poststructuralist criticism of the novel — is a shift from the classical view of the novel as a passive reflector of social change (the "mirror walking along a roadway") to one that casts the novel as an active agent in the formation of the discourse that shapes all subjectivity, including gender. It should also be noted that gender criticism in this vein has reestablished a clear connection to the literary-critical feminism of the 1960s and 1970s, which shared its assumption that fiction has social implications.

Once criticism adopted this sort of cultural emphasis, as it has since roughly 1985, it has became apparent that no special privilege need be accorded to the "serious" novel; indeed, in the construction of subjectivity, popular novels might well be equally powerful. Nineteenth-century novelists such as Fanny Fern (1811–1872), Susan Warner (1819–1885), E. D. E. N. Southworth (1819–1899), Maria Cummins (1827–1866), and Charlotte Yonge (1823–1901) became newly popular objects of critical study, and some feminist critics began to question whether even mass-market genres such as the domestic romance might not be in some way liberating for women readers.[13] In their sophisticated readings of works dismissed as trivial and emotionally stultifying by a long line of (usually) male critics, they demonstrated one of the many ways in which feminism has been able to open new vistas in literary criticism.

GAY AND LESBIAN STUDIES

The rise and partial institutionalization of gay and lesbian studies in the 1980s has in some ways mirrored the trajectory of African American studies and then feminist studies, though it has proceeded more rapidly. It can be argued that the disempowerment of these sexually defined groups was even more extreme, though: in theory, mainstream thought in America and Europe in the twentieth century saw nothing "wrong" with being a woman or being black, as long as each group kept in its place, whereas to be gay or lesbian was defined as pathological. Gay and lesbian studies thus begins with the recognition of what Adrienne Rich calls the "compulsory heterosexuality" of our culture and opposes to that an assertion of every person's right to his or her own sexual orientation. The first stage of the literary-critical movement (which, like feminism, coincided with a broader social movement)[14] was the recognition of how many canonical writers had been gay or lesbian. The lists varied but usually included Sappho (c. 650 B.C.), Plato, Christopher Marlowe (1564–1592), Walt Whitman, Arthur Rimbaud, Oscar Wilde, Willa Cather, Marcel Proust, H.D., E. M. Forster, Gertrude Stein, Virginia Woolf, Djuna Barnes, W. H. Auden, Christopher Isherwood, and Elizabeth Bishop (1911–1979). It would not be a stretch to include writers whose sexuality was never directly expressed (perhaps because of social pressure), such as Henry James, Emily Dickinson, and G. B. Shaw. Disagreement about definitions is inevitable here, but lists of bisexual authors often include Shakespeare, Lord Byron, Herman Melville, D. H. Lawrence (potentially, despite his homophobia), Katherine Mansfield, Elizabeth Bowen, Somerset Maugham (1874–1965), and many others. This does not count contemporary writers, of whom, because of loosening social restrictions, a larger proportion are known to be gay or lesbian.

At least until World War II, most of the novels treating gay and lesbian protagonists that succeeded in finding publication followed the pattern of Radclyffe Hall's (1886–1943) notorious *Well of Loneliness* (1928), in which the lesbian protagonist is romantically doomed, or of Forster's equally painful *Maurice* (1971; written c. 1914) with its hopeful but (according to Forster) unconvincing ending. The vicious trial of Oscar Wilde and the prosecution of *The Well* for obscenity made it clear why most such literary works never saw daylight. The contemporary period has produced more affirmative novels, of which Rita Mae Brown's (b. 1944) *Rubyfruit Jungle* (1973) is the best-known example. The communal "mythos" of the contemporary lesbian novel is analyzed in Bonnie Zimmerman's *The Safe Sea of Women: Lesbian Fiction, 1969–1989* (1990). Zimmerman makes an implicit argument for the quality and overall interest of these lesser-known contemporary works which, like similar novels exploring gay male life, reflect an experience in a way not possible earlier.

Another branch of gay and lesbian criticism is devoted to interrogating the previous silence on the subject, with the assumption that gay and lesbian experience is indeed represented in earlier novels, but indirectly, in "coded" form. Some of this critical activity resembles early Freudian criticism, in which critics found "repressed homosexuality" in the works of Lawrence, or a neo-Freudian critic such as Leslie Fiedler identified disguised homoerotic relationships throughout classic American literature.[15] A different kind of approach is offered by, for example, Karla Jay's rereading of modernism with the assumption that "lesbian modernists encoded lesboerotic content and language and foregrounded issues of gender identification in content as well as in experimental language." Jay argues that, sometimes using disguised lesbian content in traditional forms, sometimes using traditional content in experimental forms that challenged patriarchy, works by Willa Cather, Radclyffe Hall, Natalie Clifford Barney (1876–1972), Renée Vivien (1877–1909), and Elizabeth Bowen seem more convincingly modernist than literary scholarship has admitted.[16] Her argument here is somewhat parallel to Bonnie Kime Scott's thesis of a feminist modernism.

A generalized form of gay and lesbian literary criticism that might be better described as a particular branch of cultural studies has been named by its proponents "queer theory," in a gesture of affirmatively reclaiming a term of insult. Queer theory, as Teresa de Lauretis explains, can be seen as an attempt to construct a concept of gay and lesbian sexualities in a way that offers an alternative to the notion of deviancy or of being "marginal with regard to a dominant, stable form of sexuality (heterosexuality) against which it would be defined." Instead, the attempt is to define male and female homosexualities as "social and cultural forms in their own right," which may be "imaged as forms of resistance to cultural homogenization."[17] Influenced both by deconstruction and by Foucault's radical questioning of cultural "givens," contemporary queer theory and gender studies often adopt a philosophical position that questions the "natural" quality of bipolar sexuality and replaces it with a continuum. Eve Kosovsky Sedgwick has asked why,

> of the very many dimensions along which the genital activity of one person can be differentiated from another (dimensions that include preference for certain acts, certain zones or sensations, certain physical types, . . . a certain number of participants, etc. etc. etc.), precisely one, the gender of object choice, emerged from the turn of the century, and has remained, as *the* dimension denoted by the now ubiquitous category of "sexual orientation."[18]

This sort of questioning of the cultural mechanics that have produced contemporary society is fundamental to queer theory. It reinterprets not only sexuality, but identity itself.

With queer theory we have come a considerable distance from direct considerations of the novel as genre, although prose fiction is still the most common form of discourse to be analyzed by critical approaches that declare themselves competent to analyze any form. Yet the effect of such a shifting of fundamental assumptions is especially pronounced for the reading of novels, in which social norms are so complexly encoded (and in which the "marriage plot" is still so pervasive). Like feminism — or, for that matter, like postcolonial criticism — gender studies has been both affected and informed by the linguistic emphasis of Continental criticism, so that where formal experiments and disruptions in a novel for a feminist might suggest a struggle against patriarchal phallogocentrism, for a postcolonial critic they might denote protest against imperial hegemony and for a queer theorist the resistance to compulsory gender identifications that are woven into both the language and the traditional forms of fiction. Further, we should remember that all these fields are beginning to explore the implications of a new concern to historicize particulars rather than to generalize about universals. The results of these transmutations in the criticism of the novel are just beginning to be felt, and no doubt the dialogue will continue. As we think over the history of criticism and its possibilities, it is well to recall Mikhail Bakhtin's affirmation that "there is neither a first nor a last word"; even forgotten ideas are continually reborn and renewed, so that "nothing is absolutely dead: every meaning will have its homecoming festival."[19]

NOTES

1. Wayne Booth, "Freedom of Interpretation: Bakhtin and the Challenge of Feminist Criticism," *Bakhtin: Essays and Dialogues on His Work,* ed. Gary Saul Morson (Chicago: U of Chicago P, 1986) 147; originally published in *Critical Inquiry* 9 (Sept. 1982).

2. Janet Todd, *Feminist Literary History* (New York: Routledge, 1988) 30.

3. Ellen Moers, *Literary Women: The Great Writers* (New York: Doubleday, 1976); Patricia Meyer Spacks, *The Female Imagination* (New York: Knopf, 1975).

4. Elaine Showalter, *A Literature of Their Own: British Women Novelists from Brontë to Lessing* (Princeton: Princeton UP, 1977) 13.

5. Sandra Gilbert and Susan Gubar, *No Man's Land: The Place of the Woman Writer in the Twentieth Century, vol. 1, The War of the Words* (New Haven: Yale UP, 1987).

6. Bonnie Kime Scott, ed. *The Gender of Modernism: A Critical Anthology* (Bloomington: Indiana UP, 1990).

7. Annis Pratt et al., *Archetypal Patterns in Women's Fiction* (Bloomington: Indiana UP, 1981) 168.

8. Rachel Blau DuPlessis, *Writing beyond the Ending: Narrative Strategies of Twentieth-Century Writers* (Bloomington: Indiana UP, 1985).

9. Judith Kegan Gardner, "On Female Identity and Writing by Women," *Writing and Sexual Difference,* ed. Elizabeth Abel (Chicago: U of Chicago P, 1982) 179, 182.

10. Todd 50.

11. Alice Jardine, *Gynesis: Configurations of Women and Modernity* (Ithaca: Cornell UP, 1985); Toril Moi, *Sexual/Textual Politics: Feminist Literary Theory* (New York: Methuen, 1985); Shari Benstock, *Textualizing the Feminine: On the Limits of Genre* (Norman: U of Oklahoma P, 1991).

12. Nancy Armstrong, *Desire and Domestic Fiction: A Political History of the Novel* (New York: Oxford UP, 1987) 23, 26.

13. See Tania Modleski, *Loving with a Vengeance: Mass-Produced Fantasies for Women* (Hamden: Archon, 1982), and Janice Radway, *Reading the Romance: Woman, Patriarchy, and Popular Literature* (Chapel Hill: U of North Carolina P, 1984).

14. The gay liberation movement is often traced to 1969 when gay men and lesbians fought back against a police raid of a Greenwich Village bar called the Stonewall Inn.

15. Leslie Fiedler, *Love and Death in the American Novel* (New York: Criterion, 1960), available in various reissues.

16. Karla Jay, "Lesbian Modernism: (Trans)Forming the (C)Anon," *Professions of Desire: Lesbian and Gay Studies in Literature,* ed. George E. Haggerty and Bonnie Zimmerman (New York: MLA, 1995) 73.

17. Teresa de Lauretis, "Queer Theory: Lesbian and Gay Sexualities: An Introduction," *Differences* 5.2 (1991): iii.

18. Eve Kosofsky Sedgwick, *Epistemology of the Closet* (Berkeley: U of California P, 1990) 8.

19. M. M. Bakhtin, *Speech Genres and Other Late Essays,* trans. Vern W. McGee (Austin: U of Texas P, 1986) 170.

Glossary:
Elements of the Novel

To include in a glossary some basic terms used in discussing the novel seemed innocent enough until fairly recently. But once we begin to question basic assumptions about the novel (or indeed literature in general) we also begin to suspect that setting out simple definitions of basic literary terms is a way of begging the important questions that literature can raise. There are no disinterested definitions, in literature or in life. Avant-garde writing, writing by women, writing by people of color or by the colonized, and in some ways modern writing itself all frequently put into question our inherited ideas about plot, character, narration, and even the fundamental question of what constitutes literature.[1]

In the book up to this point our approach has been predominantly *historical,* as we surveyed the development of theories of fiction or the rise of modernism, postmodernism, and a group of recent critical approaches. In this glossary, in contrast, our emphasis is *formal,* stressing terminology and the logical analysis of literary elements. But there is nothing absolute about this information, and what follows is less a list of definitions than a series of discussions of terms most literary specialists take to be elemental. These discussions are meant to reflect the changing ways that serious readers and authors, as well as academic critics, have read novels.

CHARACTER

A person we seem to encounter in a narrative (or drama). We generally evaluate such characters somewhat as we do actual persons, by their speech and actions. Unlike in real life, though, in a novel sometimes we have privileged access to the character's most private thoughts, and we frequently have the benefit of the implied or explicit attitude of the narrator as well.

E. M. Forster in *Aspects of the Novel* (1927) distinguishes between "flat" characters, who are relatively unchanging and one-dimensional, and "round" characters, who develop during the narrative and may well surprise us with their actions. "Round" characters are complex, are seen from many sides and in many contexts, and in general are supposed to mirror the psychological depth we attribute to actual human beings. "Flat" characters, like the conventionally recognized stereotypes we call character "types," are none of these things and often have a single dominant interest or characteristic. Frequently they have a verbal or descriptive "tag" associated with them, like Bertrand Welch in Kingsley Amis's novel *Lucky Jim* (1954), whose affected accent causes him to end his sentences "you sam" when he means to say "you see." A more traditional example is the minor character in Dickens's *David Copperfield* (1849–1850) who frequently volunteers, "Barkis is willin'." The critic Thomas Docherty makes a related distinction when he suggests that characters may be "static" if their "existence is entirely accounted for in the fiction; this character is simply a function of the plot or design of the whole and cannot step outside the bounds of the fiction." What Docherty calls a "kinetic" character, in contrast, "is one who is able to be absent from the text; this character's motivation extends beyond that which is merely necessary for the accomplishment of the design of the plot, and he or she 'moves' in other spheres than the one we are engaged in reading."[2] A round or a kinetic character is not necessarily aesthetically better than a flat or a static one; literature uses different systems or orders of characterization, so that it would be pointless to compare, say, Aeneas with Don Quixote, or Quixote with Henry James's Isabel Archer, or Isabel Archer with Toni Morrison's Sula in order to determine which is the "best" character. All of these are remarkably successful characters who inhabit very different literary modes.

Although we are probably incapable of thinking about character — in novels or in life — without our inherited Western presumption that each individual is unlike all others, paradoxically we are equally unable to escape the use of stereotypes in doing so. The ancient Greeks recognized that they had character types in their drama (such as the "eiron" — a

self-deriding figure — or the "alazon" — an imposter and braggart). In
the Middle Ages scholars developed a theory of the "humors" in which
people's personality types were classified as "choleric," "sanguine," "mel-
ancholy," or "phlegmatic" depending on whether the fluid of yellow bile,
blood, black bile, or phlegm, respectively, was dominant in their bodies.
A modern variant of such classification is the psychologist W. H. Sheldon's
"phenotypes," popular during the 1940s, according to which a person was
either a "mesomorph" (muscular, active, and assertive), an "endomorph"
(fat, self-indulgent, and passive), or an "ectomorph" (slender and spiritual or intellectual).[3] The nineteenth century was rife with theories of
character and with popular interest in the subject. The first mass-market
paperbacks were 120-page "physiologies" marketed in Paris in the 1840s
describing types such as "The Englishman in Paris," "The Drinker," "The
Salesgirl," "The Stevedore," and so forth. A debate between "nature" and
"nurture" as a causative influence structured much of the discussion of
character. The writer Émile Zola, who saw himself as a scientist, insisted
that his novels were like experiments — he filled them with characters
with a given heredity, placed them in a given social situation, and simply
observed the inevitable results.

What kinds of characters appear in prose narratives and in dramas depends in part on the expectations of an audience. During the eighteenth
century much credence was given to the notion that literature should offer clear-cut examples of virtuous persons to emulate and, perhaps, vil-
lains to condemn. Fielding's Squire Allworthy was obviously one of the
former, Dickens's Gradgrind one of the latter. The nineteenth century
did not abandon this notion but gradually put a greater premium on the
vividness and "lifelikeness" of a variety of characters. Novelists were praised
for their accurate and wide-ranging eye. They did not necessarily abandon the habit of giving their characters meaningful names, but readers
could not always trust the implications of the names. Thus Thomas Hardy's
Angel Clare might not be admirable in all respects, and James Joyce's
Stephen Dedalus might fall like Icarus instead of flying like his name-
sake. Postmodern novelists such as Thomas Pynchon might endow characters with names like Oedipa Maas and Benny Profane — unlikely enough
names whose implications were mysterious or ambiguous.

By the twentieth century, some artists had grown tired of what they
saw as the artificial and mechanical creation of a gallery of distinct characters. "On or about December, 1910, human character changed," wrote
Virginia Woolf half-seriously, resolving to abandon the conventional realistic character in her novels. Most modernists agreed with her about the
inadequacy of character as it was traditionally conceived in fiction, but

not necessarily because they felt it unimportant. Henry James had argued that the novelist's ability to portray psychological depth was among literature's most important functions; but, many modernists believed, such depth could be represented only by revolutionary techniques such as stream of consciousness narration. This might lead to the representation of character in a more profound way than was done previously, but ordinary readers sometimes felt that character as they knew it was simply being abandoned.

If modernist writers see character as a more complex, contradictory, and tentative matter than do their nineteenth-century predecessors, those writers we call postmodern often seem to reject the idea of novelistic characters outright. Kafka's and Beckett's characters usually appear to have relatively little individual psychology; like the near-anonymous K of *The Castle* (1926) or the protagonist of *Molloy* (1955), they *are* essentially their *situation*. Often, even if they pretend to establish ordinary novelistic characters, postmodern authors then assiduously destroy the illusion. John Fowles paradoxically both destroys and reinforces novelistic verisimilitude in chapter 13 of *The French Lieutenant's Woman* (1969), when the narrator interrupts the action to discuss his inability as author to force his characters to do what he has planned for them to do. Characters in the French *nouveau roman* ("new novel") of the 1960s tend to have very little depth. In Robbe-Grillet's *Jealousy* (1957), whoever is watching the house is not characterized at all, whereas a spot on a wall within is described for many paragraphs without any apparent motivation in the book's plot.

Meanwhile, critics of the 1970s, influenced by the thinking of the Russian formalists about folklore, sometimes replaced the idea of character with the idea of plot "functions," so that what an "actor" did in a narrative came to be seen as a defining characteristic within that narrative. The narratologist A. J. Greimas, in fact, distinguishes between the *actor*, a recognizable character who performs a particular function in a sequence of events, and the *actant*, a term referring to that character's functional position; thus several characters may make up a single actant, from a narratological perspective. Contemporary narratologists have greatly sophisticated the study of character, starting with the belief that character is most usefully analyzed from an appreciation of how it works within narratives rather than as a sort of indirect psychology. James Phelan has proposed a model for analyzing character that suggests we see it as an element of narrative composed of *mimetic*, *thematic*, and *synthetic* aspects. The mimetic aspect refers to the character's verisimilitude, his or her probability and coherence as a person; the thematic aspect refers to the character as representative of particular ideas or a particular group that has

significance within the narrative; and the synthetic aspect refers to character as an artificial, textual construct. The relationship among these three
aspects varies from work to work, depending on what is emphasized by
the unfolding narrative. We may find our focus mostly upon the mimetic
aspects of character in a conventionally realistic narrative, whereas a modernist narrative may demand more attention to the relationship between
a given character and the narrator and between these two and ourselves
reading. Or the very notion of character may come under attack in the
postmodern narrative, throwing most of our attention to the synthetic
aspect. Phelan points out that characters have what he terms *dimensions*,
or the potential to be meaningful in each of the three spheres, and also
functions, or realizations of that potential within the actual narrative.[4]

In general, contemporary study of character has de-emphasized traditional humanist perspectives on the issue, just as much "advanced" contemporary fiction features characters with little apparent psychological
depth. At least some of this change in novelistic criticism and practice is
related to a sense that character as it is traditionally conceived, both in
life and in art, is a sham and that the "unified self" of classical psychology
is an illusion. (See chap. 3.)

NOVEL

Definitions

A novel is a kind of written *narrative*, the recounting of a series of
events. The majority of the world's narratives have been (and still are)
oral. The first rigorous attempt to study narratives from a theoretical standpoint was made by Russian formalist critics such as Vladimir Propp and
Viktor Shklovski, who studied folktales and jokes as well as long poems,
stories, and novels. The relationship of the novel in particular to narratives in general and to its narrative predecessors is not clear. Narratives
need not be fictional, and since the novel often masquerades as "true,"
the genre's relationship to factual narratives is also a vexed question.

One way of deciding what the novel *is* is to decide where it *comes
from*. The critic Lennard Davis classifies theories of the novel's origin
into three groups: the evolutionary, the osmotic, and the convergent. *Evolutionary* theories argue that, for example, the prose romance gradually
became more realistic until it turned into something like the form we
recognize as a novel. *Osmotic* theories argue that literary forms "absorb"
changes in the structure of society and change accordingly; thus the rise
of the bourgeoisie and the new interest in individualism following the

Renaissance can be said to have produced the novel. Theories of *convergence* argue that different genres (the romance, the biography, and the picaresque narrative, for instance) come together to form the new genre of the novel. Clearly one of the issues on which such arguments depend is the larger question of what causes changes in aesthetic genres.[5]

In any case, most major theorists of the novel have observed that it is a hybrid form, a mixture of preceding genres. Robert Scholes and Robert Kellogg have stressed the idea that the novel as a form is dependent on the spread of writing, and with it the solidification in popular consciousness of a distinction between fact and fiction. Because its roots are in such a variety of narrative forms, from epic and romance through the character sketch, the allegory, and saints' lives, these critics see the novel as an "unstable compound, inclining always to break down into its constituent elements."[6] Perhaps the critic Mikhail Bakhtin, writing before and independently of Scholes and Kellogg, took this approach furthest, arguing that the novel is a paradoxical antigeneric genre that refuses to be circumscribed by the laws of literary genres (see chap. 1).

Simply approaching the question pragmatically, we might find that the safest definition is something like "an extended work of prose fiction," though even that raises questions: How extended? What do we mean by fiction and how can we tell it from fact? How do we distinguish "prose" from "poetry" if much twentieth-century poetry is unrhymed and unmetered? Setting aside such basic problems for the moment, we can observe that a novel is generally longer than a novella and considerably longer than a short story. It is usually distinguished from the long verse narratives (that is, rhymed and metered stories) of writers like Geoffrey Chaucer (c. 1342–1400), Edmund Spenser (c. 1552–1599), and John Milton (1608–1674), through Alfred, Lord Tennyson in the nineteenth century; critics usually see the novel as displacing this form. Within the tradition of realism — and most novels are written within that tradition — the novel attempts to give the impression of being a factual narrative without actually being one.

Kinds of Novel

So long as we stay within the predominantly realistic tradition, we can add a great many other qualifiers to the definition of the novel. It generally has a single major plot and often a group of relatively minor subplots. Usually there is a single *protagonist* (the main character) or group of protagonists who are importantly involved in the series of related events that make up the novel's plot. Sometimes we distinguish between the *novel of incident,* in which the main focus is on the novel's events, and the *novel of character*, in which the main focus is on the major protagonist's reactions and development; but in practice these two kinds are likely to be blended. Because, especially in the nineteenth century, the novel concentrated so frequently on the experience and development of a single central character, the German terms *Bildungsroman* and *Erziehungsroman* became current, both referring to the "novel of formation" or "novel of education." The most frequently cited early example of this is Johann Wolfgang von Goethe's (1749–1832) *Wilhelm Meister's Apprenticeship* (1795–1796). Among the most popular recent Bildungsromans are J. D. Salinger's *Catcher in the Rye* (1951) and Alice Walker's (b. 1944) *The Color Purple* (1982). A more specialized novel of development, the *Künstlerroman* is specifically concerned with the life of an artist. Perhaps the most famous of these is James Joyce's *Portrait of the Artist as a Young Man* (1916).

These terms all build upon *roman*, the word for "novel" in several European languages, which is also the root of the English word *romance*. In British and American usage the romance, which can be in prose or in verse, is sometimes distinguished from the novel because it involves heroic and/or villainous characters — in any case, figures larger than life — in unrealistic situations whose significance is symbolic. *Romance novels*, which can be said to cross the romance with the novel, include flamboyant adventure narratives like Alexandre Dumas's (1824–1895) *The Count of Monte Cristo* (1844–1845) or Robert Louis Stevenson's (1850–1894) *Treasure Island* (1883). Today we often reserve the term *romance novels* to mean highly stereotyped books whose intended audience is female and whose plot involves the romantic relationship between a female protagonist and a male figure. This is the most restrictive sense of the term *romance*; in its broadest sense, the term can include most important American novels, including those of Cooper, Hawthorne, Melville, Twain, and Faulkner. These can be called *romances* in contrast to the *novel proper*, which is predominantly concerned with the situation of a protagonist in society, exemplified by the works of Austen, Thackeray, and George Eliot.

The prose romance of the Middle Ages was one source of the novel. Another was the *picaresque narrative*, which emerged in sixteenth-century Spain; perhaps the greatest picaresque narrative is Miguel de Cervantes's *Don Quixote* (1605). The picaresque narrative involves the loosely linked adventures of a rogue, a likable delinquent who is generally interested only in survival and in satisfying his baser desires. *Don Quixote* is far more complex than this, and many critics would call it a novel proper with a heavy picaresque element; such novels have continuously appeared, from Daniel Defoe's *Moll Flanders* (1722), sometimes called the first novel in English, to Saul Bellow's *Adventures of Augie March* (1953). A rather grotesque recent example is Kathy Acker's *Don Quixote: Which Was a Dream* (1986). Jack Kerouac's *On the Road* (1957) can be called both picaresque and a Künstlerroman, although it stretches both terms. If we assume that the key element of a picaresque narrative is that its plot is episodic — a more or less random series of incidents — rather than architecturally structured, then most adventure novels are picaresque.

Another candidate as the first novel in English is Samuel Richardson's *Pamela* (1740). Richardson was compiling for publication a collection of model letters for various occasions as he was writing the book, and it occurred to him to present his fiction through a series of letters, or "epistles." From this we derive the term *epistolary novel*. There are, of course, disadvantages to the epistolary method, which Richardson continued to employ in his hugely successful multivolume novel *Clarissa* (1747–1748). So that Richardson can maintain both immediacy and suspense, at times his heroines find themselves writing in absurd circumstances letters they should have no hope of mailing. In Henry Fielding's parody *Shamela* (1741), the heroine continues to write as her seducer is climbing into her bed. Despite such artificialities the form has never died out. John Barth bade farewell to all the characters from his earlier novels in a huge epistolary novel entitled *Letters* (1979), while in Nick Bantock's (b. 1949) surprise best-seller *Griffin and Sabine: An Extraordinary Correspondence* (1991) the author has included a physically complete exchange of letters, down to the envelopes and samples of the correspondents' artwork.

Types or genres of the novel can be multiplied indefinitely. Any current bookstore divides popular novels into subgroups according to readers' interests — western, Gothic, science fiction, mystery, horror, romance, and so forth. For some of these, such as the Gothic, there is historical background. The Gothic novel emerged as early as the eighteenth century, with Horace Walpole's *The Castle of Otranto* (1764). The modern incarnation maintains many of the genre's original features — the haunted castles, the horrifying secrets, the brooding presence of the past, and the permeation of ordinary experience with the supernatural. Other types, such as the mystery novel, are for the most part late-nineteenth-century and twentieth-century forms. The *historical novel* is set at a time considerably before the time of writing. The genre was begun by Walter Scott in the early nineteenth century with *Ivanhoe* (1819), set in the reign of Richard I; Margaret Mitchell's (1832–1918) *Gone with the Wind* (1936) is set during the American Civil War and afterward. Although the form has been used by writers with high literary aims, such as Ford Madox Ford and E. L. Doctorow (b. 1931), today it is more likely to be employed by writers of popular romances. Of course, some contemporary writing denies any distinction between "serious" and "popular" literature. A. S. Byatt's *Possession* (1990) is partly a historical romance that is also both "serious" literature and very popular.

More academic categories include the *roman à thèse*, or "thesis novel," written didactically to argue a social thesis. Harriet Beecher Stowe's *Uncle Tom's Cabin* (1852), with its attack on slavery, is perhaps the most famous of these. More recently, John D. MacDonald's (1916–1986) best-selling novel *Condominium* (1977) combined suspense and entertainment with a serious desire to reform building practices on Florida's coasts. In the *roman à clef,* or "novel with a key," the characters and plot are thinly disguised versions of actual people and events; the anonymously authored *Primary Colors* (1996), for instance, fictionalizes the first Clinton campaign. The *roman-fleuve*, which suggests "river novel" or "novel of flow," is a sequence of novels that can stand alone but that deal with some of the same characters or happenings. Balzac's gigantic *Human Comedy* (first collected 1842–1846) is a well-known example; a British series is Anthony Powell's *A Dance to the Music of Time* (1951–1975), which includes twelve novels. Faulkner's novels in his series about the fictional Yoknapatawpha County can be so designated, although we might use the term *saga novel* if we wished to stress the novels' dependence on a single family for their coherence. John Galsworthy used that term in his *Forsyte Saga* series (1906–1935). But in fact there is little agreement among critics as to either the terminology or the aesthetics of works of fiction longer than a single novel.

Nearly every category of factual narrative, such as biography, autobiography, travel tale, and history, has a corresponding fictive form in the novel, and many of the classical genres are represented by novelistic forms as well. Many famous novels are also "satires," such as George Orwell's *Animal Farm* (1945), while the relatively plotless and highly wrought narratives of some modern and postmodern authors have been called "lyrical novels." Novels that seem to pay considerable attention to their own fictionality are sometimes called *metafictions*.

PLOT

The plot of a narrative is, most simply, the series of events and actions ordered by that narrative. In his *Poetics* Aristotle considers plot the most important aspect of a work, and he observes that plots have a beginning, middle, and end. Though we can generally distinguish easily enough between, for example, plot and character, we must also recognize that it can be difficult to describe events and actions independent of the actors and situation. Henry James in "The Art of Fiction" (1888) warned against considering the elements of fiction in isolation from one another. "What is character but the determination of incident?" he asked. "What is incident but the illustration of character?" Especially in a *psychological novel*, plot and character can be said to illuminate one another almost to the point of defining one another. Plot and setting can merge as well. In Kate Chopin's story "The Storm" (1898), the storm that seems to drive the lovers together may be simply the setting or it may be a major element of the plot.

The novelist E. M. Forster in his influential study *Aspects of the Novel* (1927) claims that "The king died and then the queen died" is a *story*. "The king died and then the queen died of grief" is a *plot*.[7] In other words, a plot is distinguished from a mere series of events by causality. Most critics today also prefer to distinguish between a novel's story — the book's events in chronological order, as they might be abstracted from the book — and its plot — the events *as the novel presents them*. The Russian formalist critics termed the former the *sjuzhet* and the latter the *fabula*. More recently, Seymour Chatman has made a very similar distinction between *story* and *discourse*.

Although in many novels story and plot coincide, in a surprising number they do not. Mystery stories, for instance, usually withhold full revelation of the initial act — a murder by a particular villain — until the end. Dickens, like many popular authors, frequently ends one chapter on a "cliffhanger" note of suspense only to follow another plot line entirely in the succeeding chapter. And modernist authors are notorious for playing with story sequence in their plots. Henry James is so vague and indirect about his revelation of story events that for years an edition of *The Ambassadors* (1903) transposed two chapters without anyone's noticing.

In *The Good Soldier* (1915), Ford Madox Ford's narrator-character claims he will reconstruct the events he has lived through just as he might if he were sitting opposite a sympathetic soul in a cottage at night, rambling; and indeed what follows is a narrative crammed with chronological twists and turns, anticipations and recollections, evasions and detours. Much of our task as readers is simply to reconstruct some sort of linear narrative out of the confusion produced by his way of telling the story. Narratologists point out that a narrator can break the sequence of temporal recounting by suddenly referring to past events in a *flashback* or *analepsis*; or he may refer forward in time in a *flashforward* or *prolepsis*. Narratologists suggest that in the direct presentation of a *scene*, the time of telling and the time of happening are roughly equivalent, whereas in *summary* the former is much less than the latter, and in *ellipsis* a series of events may be passed over altogether.

These are all measures of *duration*, or time of telling, in a narrative. We may also distinguish between *unique* and *repeated* events; some analysts refer to events that occur repeatedly but are narrated once as *iterative*, since they have a special scenic force ("Every day he passed by the glittering stream on his way to the mill, and it seemed to him . . ."). Yet it is a measure of the novel's richness that among its multitude of events we are often uncertain of the most significant, or even of their correct sequence. Mark Twain seems especially to appreciate this lifelike element of chaos in novels, including his own. A note inserted in the beginning of *Adventures of Huckleberry Finn* (1885) reads, "Persons attempting . . . to find a moral in [this story] will be banished; persons attempting to find a plot in it will be shot." Then again, it may be that Twain was only acknowledging the awkwardness of the book's final third. Some critics have suggested that in *Huckleberry Finn's* conclusion Twain was mistakenly trying to complete an "adventure plot" while his book's "real plot," which was a mythic journey, had already been realized.[8]

Parts of the Plot

Discussing tragedy, Aristotle spoke of the initial *exposition* of the situation, usually involving some sort of conflict or potential conflict; this is followed by a period of *rising action* in which *complications* are introduced. The action comes to a head in the *climax*, the point at which something important must be resolved for the protagonist. The climax may coincide with or be quickly followed by the *crisis*, in which the shape of the future is made clear. Then follows the period of *falling action* leading to what later critics call the *denouement*, or outcome (a term from the French, literally meaning "unknotting"). An alternative term for this is *resolution*.

The German critic Gustav Freytag describes the "shape" of this model as a pyramid; actually, it is more of a skewed, inverted V. Clearly this model, which originally described classical tragedy, has limited validity for a form as various as the novel — novels with a strong picaresque element, for example, will not be described by it because a random series of episodes may stop at any time or continue indefinitely. Still, critics of fiction often use this terminology, along with Aristotelian terms such as the *peripeteia*, or reversal in the protagonist's fortune, and the *anagnorisis*, or discovery, which may lead to the reversal. A more modern term for the moment of sudden spiritual illumination that may mark a story's psychological climax is the *epiphany*.

Some critics distinguish between what Henry James called "telling" in a narrative and "showing" — between the parts of a novel that advance the plot and those that represent the words of the characters or describe the setting. More formally, we can adopt Plato's terms in book 3 of *The Republic*, where he speaks of *diegesis*, which represents action in the words of the writer, and *mimesis*, which represents action in the words of the characters. We might take diegesis to refer to any part of a novel's discourse in which the author's (or narrator's) own voice is predominant, mimesis to refer to parts where characters' voices are predominant; or we might associate diegesis with the function of advancing the plot (whether through reported action, summary, or even commentary), and mimesis with the function of establishing the illusion of reality. Clearly in many instances these functions and voices overlap, and some critics, such as Bakhtin, feel that a novel is working properly only when they *are* overlapping.

In addition to distinguishing between the modes of presentation of events, we also may distinguish the critical events from the less important ones. What perspective allows us to say that the movie *Clueless* (1995) has the same plot as Jane Austen's *Emma* (1816) or that *Apocalypse Now* (1979) has the same plot as Conrad's *Heart of Darkness* (1902), despite their stunningly different surfaces? Narratologists today try to distinguish between *kernel* events — those that raise important possibilities and mark significant divergences within the sequence of events — and *satellite* events, which fill in the outline of a sequence mostly by elaborating on the kernel events. As Steven Cohan and Linda Shires put it, "Since kernels are the points of action that advance a sequence, they cannot be removed, reordered, or replaced without substantially altering that sequence. Satellites, by contrast, can be omitted, reordered, or replaced (by other satellites) without revising the sequence." Kernels are, so to speak, the skeleton of the story, satellites the flesh.[9]

Kinds of Plot

Numerous attempts have been made to describe the major kinds of plot; the more an analyst is willing to gloss over differences in detail, the fewer the types of plot he or she will identify. The French critic Georges Polti thought there were just thirty-six kinds of dramatic situation; James Joyce, who owned his book, defiantly proceeded to write a play whose plot was not among the thirty-six. Lord Raglan in *The Hero* (1936) argues that there is a single "basic" myth whose "universal plot" is shared by all cultures, involving a hero's journey and trial. Joseph Campbell in *The Hero with a Thousand Faces* (1949) offers a somewhat different version of what he terms the *monomyth*. Novels may reflect such mythic patterns, but because of their usually mundane realism they are less likely to do so than are, say, romances. Northrop Frye in *Anatomy of Criticism* (1957) argues that there are four main kinds of plot, with their associated "modes," corresponding to the seasons of the year. Spring is comedy, summer romance, autumn tragedy, and winter satire and irony. In this scheme the realistic novel belongs mostly to winter. Its primary mode, he observes, is ironic.

Campbell's and Frye's different varieties of *archetypal* criticism are examples of what we can call *master narratives* — attempts to explain the most significant aspects of life through a single story. Sigmund Freud and Karl Marx offer other master narratives, and in their footsteps some critics find that what is important about the plots of most novels is the way in which they work out the Oedipal drama or embody the class struggle. Clearly in a work as complex as a novel much will depend on the elements to which we choose to direct our attention when we try to identify the "essential story." A psychologist may find that a particular novel's main plot involves the painful but necessary loss of innocence for the protagonist; an anthropologist may note that the story embodies a mythic pattern of journey, trial, and renewal for the protagonist; a sociologist may be struck by the fact that the protagonist's movement from the country to the city shapes his or her experience; a Marxist historian may feel that the narrative fundamentally celebrates the rise of a member of the petite bourgeoisie at the expense of the lower classes. These may all be readings of the same novel, although we can debate whether all these readers have experienced the same "plot."

At the other extreme of critical perspective, several commentators have suggested that plot in the modern sense of the word, which includes implications of uniqueness and possible variety, emerges only around the Renaissance. The emergence of plot thus is part of the process of secularization and abandonment of the "revealed plots" offered by the church as the only narratives worth recounting. The critic Peter Brooks has argued that in its modern meaning, *plot* always carries with it some of the implication of "conspiracy" or "intrigue":

> The organizing line of plot is more often than not some scheme or machination, a concerted plan for the accomplishment of some purpose which goes against the ostensible and dominant legalities of the fictional world, the realization of a blocked and resisted desire. Plots are not simply orga-

nizing structures, they are also intentional structures, goal-oriented and forward-moving.[10]

From Brooks's perspective, which is at root Freudian, plot mirrors the working of human desire in all its variety.

But we can also debate whether a plot of any sort is crucial to the novel. While most critics, following Aristotle, have argued that plot is fundamental in works of fiction, other approaches — and some schools of writing — minimize its importance. Certainly it is hard to describe what is important about Sterne's *Tristram Shandy* (1759–1767) in terms of plot, since it takes three of the book's eight volumes for Sterne to get around to describing the birth of his protagonist. When Henry James characterizes most novels as "loose baggy monsters," he implies that whatever skeleton they might have is not obvious under their shapeless padding of details. James does not mean this as praise, but Virginia Woolf (for one) points out that we can learn more from the "incidentals" of a novel than its framework. Plot is just one of the elements, like external descriptions and character in the conventional sense, with which she feels a modern novelist might dispense in order to capture the quality of lived experience.

Both modernist writers and postmodernists tend to follow Woolf in their relative disregard for plot. Flaubert, who anticipates the modernists in this, feels that there is something cheap about depending on obviously important or dramatic happenings in a novel (see chap. 1, pp. 12–13). What he would like to do is write "a book which would have practically no subject, or at least one in which the subject would be invisible."[11] Important or unimportant, "visible" or not, whether or not the events in a novel appear to "resolve themselves" or "come to a conclusion" is a slightly different question. At least since the 1960s, some theorists have argued that this sort of novelistic *closure* is not characteristic of more experimental works of fiction. And indeed it is difficult to say how the minimal events in a novel by Samuel Beckett, for instance, can be said to come to any resolution at all. They are more likely to trail off than to conclude: *The Unnamable* (1958) ends with the narrating protagonist's complaint "I'll never know, in the silence you don't know, you must go on, I can't go on, I'll go on."

Novels in which chronological sequence is rearranged so that we know the outcome from the beginning and also conspicuously "open" novels in which no plot resolution is achieved both call for a different perspective on the problem of what keeps readers reading. Broadly speaking, we can ask what replaces conventional plot in "plotless" novels. James Phelan has suggested using the term *progression* to refer to the movement of a narrative through time; he speaks of the *instabilities* an author may introduce, complicate, resolve, or leave unresolved in the course of a narrative. Traditional instabilities are those within the *story*, or the series of events; but there may also be instabilities of *discourse*, "instabilities — of value, belief, opinion, knowledge, expectation — between authors and/ or narrators, on the one hand, and the authorial audience on the other."[12]

This critical move toward the reader's response acknowledges that in many fictions the main action is taking place between the author (or what Wayne Booth calls the "implied author") and us, the readers, and the main "plot" may involve our developing relationship with the narrator. It may also involve our delighted or annoyed recognition of the game the author has been playing with us. There are plenty of narratives in which the author (or narrator) seems to be glorying in his or her own arbitrary power. Richard Brautigan's novel *Trout Fishing in America* (1967), which has nothing much to do with trout fishing, concludes, "Expressing a human need, I always wanted to write a book that ended with the word Mayonnaise."

The critical approach called "reader-response criticism" has developed in part to examine more closely the way actual or hypothetical readers are manipulated by texts (and in turn manipulate them). Gérard Genette approaches an aspect of this problem by suggesting the term *narratee* for the one presumably narrated to, the communicative partner of the narrator. The narratee may or may not coincide with an actual reader. A great deal of contemporary criticism is devoted to exploring the way narratives, including both novels and films, construct a "subject position" for the person reading or viewing, influencing us to adopt particular political, ethical, aesthetic, and psychological postures while we may be entirely ignorant of the subtle pressures exerted on us.

POINT OF VIEW

The perspective from which the novel is written or the way the story is told. Like most aspects of the novel, we conventionally discuss this complicated question in human terms, as if a person, or perhaps God imitating a person, were actually present, telling us a story involving other persons. Because this is not really the situation, some of the elaborate terminology that has grown up around the discussion is a bit artificial. Much of the importance attributed to point of view in the novel grew from ideas developed by Henry James in his introductions to his novels, which were collected under the title *The Art of the Novel* (1934). The critical school called the New Criticism, with its formalist emphasis, quickly adopted and elaborated James's ideas from the 1930s through the 1960s.

In keeping with this formalist emphasis, analysts of the novel often make an initial distinction between first-person narration, in which an "I" writes, and third-person narration, in which the narrator refers to the novel's characters as "he" or "she." Often overlooked is the interesting borderline case of second-person narration, in which a "you" is the actor. The effect of second-person point of view can vary; in the French "new novelist" Michel Butor's *Passing Time* (1957) it is a bit dizzying, while in Jay McInerney's *Bright Lights, Big City* (1984) it is more colloquial and "naturalized." It can be argued that after a while we read such novels by automatically translating the "you" into either "he" or "I" — but then it can also be argued that in a third-person novel with one dominant center of consciousness, we automatically translate the "he" or "she" into "I" as we identify with the protagonist.

In any case, we usually subdivide the third-person point of view into either omniscient or limited. In *omniscient* ("all-knowing") point of view, the narrator is capable of going into the minds of a variety of characters or of speaking about "future" events in the novel. Of course, few narrators demonstrate their omniscience regularly, and many are inconsistent, plunging happily into the consciousness of a character on one page and on the next avowing themselves puzzled about the same character's motives. Wayne Booth uses the term *privilege* to refer to a narrator's ability to know what could not be known by naturalistic means; complete privilege is omniscience.[13] The omniscient narrator may be *intrusive* or *editorial*, interrupting the novel's action to express opinions about the book's events and characters ("Dear Reader, do not judge poor Hortense too harshly") or even interjecting small essays on related subjects, like Melville's chapters on whaling in *Moby-Dick* (1851). In *The French Lieutenant's Woman* (1969) John Fowles, a twentieth-century author imitating a nineteenth-century one, interjects into his mock-Victorian romance small essays on Victorian culture and Marxist and Freudian analyses of the Victorian social situation. A narrator referring to himself as Fowles even indulges in discussions of his role as novelist. When he appears, badly disguised, as a character in his own novel, he probably establishes some sort of record for literary intrusiveness.

An *impersonal* or *objective* narrator, on the other hand, withholds comment on the action; probably a majority of twentieth-century authors are impersonal, on the grounds that this convention is supposed to be more realistic. Some go so far as to sacrifice any insight into the characters' thoughts and feelings. Ernest Hemingway does this in short stories such as "The Killers" (1926) as does Dashiell Hammett, whose mystery novels such as *The Maltese Falcon* (1930) establish their "hard-boiled" atmosphere partly through the scrupulous withholding of the poker-faced protagonist's sentiments. Contemporary "minimalist" writers like Raymond Carver (1938–1988) often employ this technique with somewhat different effects, as did some of the French "new novelists" of the 1950s and 1960s. We occasionally refer to impersonal narration as "fly on the wall" narration. Of course, if the narrator has no access into anyone's mind and shows no knowledge of future events, it seems odd to refer to the narration as omniscient, and many critics do not do so.

A third-person narrator that is not omniscient is said to be *limited* — limited to the perceptions and thoughts of one character (or, rarely, several characters). Narration that is strictly limited to a single character, especially if that character is the protagonist, has much the same effect as first-person narration, with the difference that the language of the narration need not be appropriate to the character. In this case we sometimes distinguish between *vision* — referring to who is doing the perceiving in a story — and *voice* — who or what is speaking. In Faulkner's story "Barn Burning" (1939) most of the action is seen through an illiterate boy's eyes, but everything, including the boy's feelings, is expressed in lush, complex Faulknerian sentences. Narratologists, following Gérard Genette, like to refer to the *focalization* of a passage. In any given passage of third-person narration there is a narrating voice, a focalizer from whose consciousness or position things are seen, and that which is focalized. It can be useful to think about the relative distance or contiguity of narrator and focalizer, narrator and focalized, and focalizer and focalized, at different points in the narration. There may be more than one focalizer in a narrative, of course, and a focalizer may well be capable of self-perception.

The subject of limited narration may be a major character in the story or a minor one. Henry James was especially fond of employing an intelligent "center of consciousness" who was on the outskirts of the story yet still involved with it. But he was reluctant to yield his own ability to comment. In *What Maisie Knew* (1897), for instance, he limits his point of view to a young girl, but more or less admits in an introduction that he cannot entirely restrict himself to her perceptions — "our own commentary constantly attends and amplifies."[14] The vision is that of a young girl, the voice that of a sophisticated adult. The Russian critic Bakhtin has observed that in fact we very seldom have a pure example of a character's own language and perceptions being employed by a novelist; usually there is some degree of collaboration between author and character (see chap. 1).

In first-person narration the speaker may be the central character, like Holden Caulfield in Salinger's *Catcher in the Rye* (1951) or like Huck Finn in *Adventures of Huckleberry Finn* (1885). It may be a secondary character, like Nick in Fitzgerald's *The Great Gatsby* (1925) or Ishmael in Melville's *Moby-Dick* (1851). It may even be a nonparticipant who is telling the story at one remove. In Conrad's *Heart of Darkness* (1902) the narrator is an unidentified person on board a ship listening to Charlie Marlow (who in turn becomes a first-person narrator) telling the story of his voyage up an African river. Almost always a first-person narrator writes *retrospectively* — that is, from a point in time, usually undetermined, later than the time of the story. This produces a kind of double consciousness in even the simplest stories, as the protagonist's reactions at the time are overlaid with his or her more mature attitudes.

Whatever his or her position, one of the first things we must decide about a characterized narrator is the degree of trust we are prepared to put in the narrator's statements. An *unreliable narrator* is one whom we have reason to distrust. For the critic Wayne Booth, there are two "axes of reliability," that of *facts* and that of *values*. In either case our judgment about the degree of reliability of a narrator is based on the *distance* that the novel implies between the narrator and the author. In Faulkner's *The Sound and the Fury* (1929) one of the several narrators, Jason Compson, is clearly a grasping, cynical manipulator who presents events in a way favorable to himself, while the idiot Benjy is unreliable in a very different way. In Ring Lardner's story "Haircut" (1925), the two axes of unreliability coincide. Part of the point of the story is that the moral obtuseness of the narrator, the barber, keeps him from seeing what we come to recognize — that his appallingly cruel friend was executed rather than being shot by mistake, as the barber believes. Sometimes the question of a narrator's reliability depends upon our reading of the novel as a whole, as with Ford Madox Ford's *The Good Soldier* (1915), in which we wonder whether we can credit the phenomenal blindness of the narrating character to what has been going on around him.

A writer may even play games with the notion of reliability, as in Agatha Christie's (1890–1976) *The Murder of Roger Ackroyd* (1926), in which the kindly doctor who narrates the story is finally revealed as the murderer: he has told us nothing untrue but has simply omitted to narrate the murder until the detective confronts him with the truth. To some extent, of course, every characterized narrator is unreliable, because a perfectly objective presentation of events is impossible. Lawrence Durrell in his four-volume sequence *The Alexandria Quartet* (1957–1960) tells the same story from a variety of different viewpoints and demonstrates how our understanding of the story (whatever that may be) changes utterly with each shift in point of view.

Another important aspect of point of view is the degree of access, or the kind of access, we have to the mind of the book's central consciousness. In third-person narration one of the most common ways of presenting experience is through the *indirect free style*, a translation of the French phrase *style indirect libre*. This refers to the way in which direct experience is conventionally paraphrased. Instead of "She turned away in dismay and thought, 'How beastly he is,'" a novelist writes in indirect free style, "She turned away in dismay. How beastly he was!" A further step into a character's consciousness is *stream of consciousness* writing, in which we are presented directly with what purports to be the running thoughts of a character, as in Mr. Bloom's breakfast in Joyce's *Ulysses* (1922): "The tea was drawn. He filled his own moustachecup, sham crown Derby, smiling. Silly Milly's birthday gift. Only five she was then. No, wait: four."[15] A passage like this, especially if it is long and has a meditative element, is often called *interior monologue*. It can work within a novel somewhat as a *soliloquy* (a spoken monologue in which the speaker is alone on stage) works in a play.

Aside from the grammatical person of narration ("I," "we," "you," "he," or "she"), there are many other ways to structure the question of narration. For instance, we might consider a spectrum of narration from fully human and specified narrators through anonymous ones to narrators whose point of view is simply not human — be it godlike, abstracted, or variable. About a third of the way into Joyce's *Ulysses* the chapters begin to be narrated in very different ways — by an unnamed barfly, by an omniscient narrator who sounds like the narrator of a sentimental romance, by another omniscient figure whose language is crammed with clichés, and so forth. One chapter is in the form of question and answer, in which both questions and responses become scientific and insanely detailed on any passing subject. Neither interlocutor seems even remotely human. And here, as with many postmodern novels, we begin to question whether the concept of point of view, with all its human baggage, actually has much relevance for the chapter. Certainly it becomes hard to speak of a "narrator" for *Ulysses* as a whole, and the critic David Hayman has suggested that we speak of an "Arranger" who controls different "narrators" in the book; others feel we can identify that figure with the (implied) author.[16]

Ulysses is still recognizably a narrative, with a recoverable plot presented more or less sequentially, but in many postmodern novels narration is no longer the book's structuring principle. The Serbo-Croatian writer

Milorad Pavić (b. 1929) calls his *Dictionary of the Khazars* (1982) a "lexicon novel," as it is organized into three main "dictionaries" each composed of alphabetical entries relating to the (imaginary) civilization of the Khazars and purporting to be drawn respectively from Christian, Islamic, and Jewish sources.[17] We may be reluctant to call this a novel — but there are in fact several "plots" that can be reconstructed from it. And once we admit that novels may have unusual modes of presentation and disturbed chronologies, it is hard to set a limit to the disturbance.

SETTING

The locale, time, and circumstance in which the action of a novel occurs. This may be quite specific, as in James Joyce's *Ulysses*, which takes place on June 16, 1904, in Dublin, Ireland, or it may be extremely vague, as in Beckett's *The Unnamable* (1958), whose protagonist sits before a featureless and vaguely illumined field, unsure whether the shapes he occasionally sees are those of men. If we admit fantasy and science fiction to our category of the novel, then the setting can be extremely detailed but imaginary, as in the Middle Earth of J. R. R. Tolkien's (1892–1973) *The Lord of the Rings* (1954–1955) or the desert planet of Frank Herbert's (1920–1986) *Dune* (1965). In fantasy and science fiction, setting, or the "background," in some respects plays the role of the foreground in the mainstream realistic novel, and so character is correspondingly minimized in those genres. If the setting of a mainstream novel is particularly important to its effect, we call the novel *atmospheric*. "Regional" writers like William Faulkner and Thomas Hardy rely on a setting that is both powerfully detailed and somewhat exotic for most of their readers, while Gothic novelists evoke particular emotions through the standard furniture of haunted castles, windswept moors, and such.

Setting can be more or less realistic, more or less conventional, more or less specified. Some murder mysteries, like those of Agatha Christie, are set in a deserted mansion that is virtually inaccessible precisely so that suspicion will be confined to a small number of characters. If we took it more seriously, we might call such a setting symbolic, as well as conventional. We certainly call the settings of D. H. Lawrence's novels symbolic, although they may also be vividly realistic: in *Women in Love* (1916) when two of the main characters have reached an extreme point in their love-hate relationship they find themselves isolated on an icy mountain. Similarly, Joseph Conrad often confines his characters to an island or a ship because, he feels, the problems he is exploring stand out with a particular "force and colouring" in the absence of "land entanglements."[18] But it is important to note that even in conventional, domestic, realistic fiction, setting and character are usually linked: to describe a person's house is to describe him or her. After Flaubert, who brilliantly realized this principle, novelists were more likely to describe characters through their surroundings than through direct description.

To speak of a novel's setting is actually to speak of something quite complex, because the action of relatively few novels can be moved to a different time and place without important changes. A setting often carries with it a mood or atmosphere; in creating a setting an author is not simply describing things but employing specific modes of description as well. It is hard to imagine broad comedy set against the brooding, dense backgrounds described by Hardy or Conrad, for example.

NOTES

1. The editor of the most important modernist magazine, *transition,* wrote in 1933: *"transition* herewith announces that in future the following words will be abolished from its pages: novel poetry verse poem ballad sonnet short story essay anthology." Eugene Jolas, "What Is the Revolution of Language?" *transition* 22 (1933): 128.

2. Thomas Docherty, *Reading (Absent) Character: Towards a Theory of Characterization in Fiction* (New York: Oxford UP, 1983) 224.

3. W. H. Sheldon, *The Varieties of Human Physique: An Introduction to Constitutional Psychology* (1940; New York: Hafner, 1963).

4. James Phelan, "Discourse, Character, and Ideology," *Reading Narrative: Form, Ethics, Ideology* (Columbus: Ohio State UP, 1989) 134.

5. Lennard Davis, *Factual Fictions: The Origins of the English Novel* (New York: Columbia UP, 1983). See the discussion in Wallace Martin, *Recent Theories of Narrative* (Ithaca: Cornell UP, 1986) 45–46.

6. Robert Scholes and Robert Kellogg, *The Nature of Narrative* (New York: Oxford UP, 1966) 15.

7. E. M. Forster, *Aspects of the Novel* (New York: Harcourt, 1927) 130.

8. René Wellek and Austin Warren, *Theory of Literature,* rev. ed. (New York: Harcourt, 1956) 217.

9. Steven Cohan and Linda M. Shires, *Telling Stories: A Theoretical Analysis of Narrative Fiction* (New York: Routledge, 1988) 54–55.

10. Peter Brooks, *Reading for the Plot: Design and Intention in Narrative* (New York: Random, 1984) 12.

11. Gustave Flaubert to Louise Colet, 16 Jan. 1852, *Documents of Modern Literary Realism,* ed. George J. Becker (Princeton: Princeton UP, 1963) 90.

12. Phelan 134.

13. Wayne Booth, *The Rhetoric of Fiction* (Chicago: U of Chicago P, 1961) 160.

14. Henry James, Preface, *What Maisie Knew* (London: Penguin, 1985) 27.

15. James Joyce, *Ulysses* (New York: Random, 1986) 51.

16. See David Hayman, Ulysses: *The Mechanics of Meaning*, rev. ed. (Madison: U of Wisconsin P, 1982).

17. Milorad Pavić, *Dictionary of the Khazars: A Lexicon Novel,* trans. Christina Pribićević-Zorić (New York: Random, 1988). This book exists in "male" and "female" versions that differ in a single paragraph.

18. Conrad to Henry Canby, 7 Apr. 1924, *Joseph Conrad: Life and Letters,* vol. 2, ed. Georges J. Aubry (Garden City: Doubleday, 1927) 342.

Bibliography: Further Reading on the Novel

1. THEORIES OF THE NOVEL

Theory of the novel and literary theory in general obviously overlap to some degree. Certainly it would be difficult to understand the ideas important writers and critics have about the novel without some acquaintance with the ideas about literature as a whole that have been entertained by our culture (and other cultures as well).

Introductions to Literary Theory and Criticism

Immediately below is a recent annotated listing of general works on critical theory, followed by sections on specific approaches.

Marshall, Donald G. *Contemporary Critical Theory: A Selective Bibliography*. New York: MLA, 1993.

The following three books are good representative anthologies of criticism, including brief explanatory sections.

Adams, Hazard, ed. *Critical Theory since Plato*. 2nd ed. Fort Worth: Harcourt, 1992.

Adams, Hazard, and Leroy Searle, eds. *Critical Theory since 1965*. Tallahassee: UP of Florida, 1986.

Davis, Robert Con, and Laurie Finke, eds. *Literary Criticism and Theory: The Greeks to the Present*. New York: Longman, 1989.

The following group of books discuss modern literary theory in ways that have particular relevance to the novel.

Booker, M. Keith. *A Practical Introduction to Literary Theory and Criticism*. White Plains: Longman, 1996. Explanatory essays on ten critical approaches, plus examples of various critical approaches applied to a group of texts, mostly novels.

Collier, Peter, and Helga Geyer-Ryan, eds. *Literary Theory Today*. Ithaca: Cornell UP, 1990. Includes feminist and psychoanalytic approaches as well as discussions of New Historicism and the relevance of race and colonialism.

Eagleton, Terry. *Literary Theory: An Introduction*. Minneapolis: U of Minnesota P, 1983. A Marxist perspective on various modern critical schools.

Hawthorn, Jeremy, ed. *Criticism and Critical Theory*. London: Arnold, 1984. Includes essays on a variety of approaches.

Leitch, Vincent B. *American Literary Criticism from the Thirties to the Eighties*. New York: Columbia UP, 1988. A survey of theories and theorists.

Schwarz, Daniel R. *The Humanistic Heritage: Critical Theories of the English Novel from James to Hillis Miller*. London: Macmillan, 1986. One of few books dealing specifically with the development of modern theories of the novel.

The following two books contain well-informed capsule summaries of approaches, terms, and critics.

Groden, Michael, and Martin Kreiswirth, eds. *The Johns Hopkins Guide to Literary Theory and Criticism*. Baltimore: Johns Hopkins UP, 1994.

Makaryk, Irena R., ed. *Encyclopedia of Contemporary Literary Theory: Approaches, Scholars, Terms*. Toronto: U of Toronto P, 1993.

The Novel and Narrative

Auerbach, Erich. *Mimesis: The Representation of Reality in Western Literature*. Trans. Willard Trask. Princeton: Princeton UP, 1953. A classic of the philological tradition of scholarship. Sophisticated analysis of realism but hostile to modernism.

Bakhtin, M. M. *The Dialogic Imagination: Four Essays*. Ed. Michael Holquist. Trans. Michael Holquist and Caryl Emerson. Austin: U of Texas P, 1981. The best introduction to Bakhtin's thought on the novel.

Barthes, Roland. *S/Z*. Trans. Richard Miller. New York: Hill and Wang,
    1974. The most famous structuralist analysis of fiction; offers
    running commentary on aspects of a story by Balzac, interspersed
    with theoretical discussion of narrative.

Booth, Wayne. *The Rhetoric of Fiction*. Chicago: U of Chicago P, 1961.
    A neo-Aristotelian perspective; a discussion of how novels work,
    establishing many of the terms for fiction's rhetorical mechanisms.

Brooks, Cleanth, and Robert Penn Warren. *Understanding Fiction*.
    New York: Holt, 1943. New Criticism applied to novels.

Edel, Leon. *The Modern Psychological Novel*. New York: Grossett,
    1959. Discussion of the modern novel in James's tradition, includ-
    ing the poetic "symbolist novel."

Forster, E. M. *Aspects of the Novel*. New York: Harcourt, 1927. The
    most inclusive statement on the novel by a major modernist
    novelist.

Frye, Northrop. *Anatomy of Criticism: Four Essays*. Princeton:
    Princeton UP, 1957. Locates the novel genre within Frye's mythic/
    anthropological system.

Halperin, John, ed. *The Theory of the Novel: New Essays*. New York:
    Oxford UP, 1974. Essays, some reflecting the impact of struc-
    turalism.

James, Henry. *The Art of the Novel*. Ed. R. P. Blackmur. New York:
    Scribner's, 1934. James's collected prefaces.

Leavis, F. R. *The Great Tradition*. New York: New York UP, 1948. The
    most influential twentieth-century British critic establishes a highly
    selective canon for the novel in England.

Lodge, David. *Language of Fiction: Essays in Criticism and Verbal
    Analysis of the English Novel*. New York: Columbia UP, 1966. An
    application of stylistics, influenced by structuralism, written by a
    comic novelist and respected critic.

Lubbock, Percy. *The Craft of Fiction*. New York: Scribner's, 1921. A
    codification and extension of Henry James's ideas about the novel.

Lukács, Gyory. *The Theory of the Novel*. Trans. Anna Bostock. Cam-
    bridge: MIT P, 1971. Published in German in 1920 by a Western
    Marxist hostile to modernism.

McKeon, Michael. *The Origins of the English Novel, 1600–1740*.
    Baltimore: Johns Hopkins UP, 1987. A revision of Watt, incorporat-
    ing more recent critical perspectives.

Martin, Wallace. *Recent Theories of Narrative*. Ithaca: Cornell UP,
    1986. Formalist, structuralist, and semiotic approaches.

Robbe-Grillet, Alain. *For a New Novel: Essays on Fiction*. Trans.
    Rich-ard Howard. New York: Grove, 1965. A combination of

criticism and manifesto by the most famous author of the "nouveau roman."

Scholes, Robert, and Robert Kellogg. *The Nature of Narrative*. New York: Oxford UP, 1966. Places novels within the broader context of narratives; a nongeneric approach, with some emphasis on the European tradition and earlier centuries.

Watt, Ian. *The Rise of the Novel*. Berkeley: U of California P, 1957. A sociological and philosophical perspective; the most influential book explaining the origin of the novel.

2. THE RISE OF MODERNISM

Although some of the more recent books listed in this section take account of the challenge to concepts of modernism and the modernist canon posed by feminism, ethnic studies, and gender studies, I have listed most books with these emphases under their respective chapters. This should not be taken to mean they are "supplementary" and the books listed here primary; if anything, a reader new to the field should probably consult a revisionary anthology like Bonnie Kime Scott's *The Gender of Modernism* (see p. 133) before reading older "standard" treatments of the period such as Walter Allen's (see p. 128).

Backgrounds

Ellmann, Richard, and Charles Feidelson, Jr. *The Modern Tradition: Backgrounds of Modern Literature*. New York: Oxford UP, 1965. A large collection of brief expository passages on subjects important in modernism by authors ranging from Blake and Wordsworth through Dylan Thomas, including substantial passages from philosophers. The readings are arranged topically.

Marwick, Arthur. *British Society since 1945. Pelican Social History of Britain*. New York: Penguin, 1982.

Stevenson, John. *British Society, 1914–1945. Pelican Social History of Britain*. New York: Penguin, 1984. In addition to consulting standard political histories, American students of the modern British novel will benefit by reading a social history such as this and Marwick above.

Williams, Raymond. *The Long Revolution*. New York: Columbia UP, 1961. Social perspective on the development of the modern condition, focusing on literacy in Great Britain.

Literary Modernism

Allen, Walter. *The Modern Novel in England and the United States.* New York: Dutton, 1964. A capable overview by a practicing novelist.

Bradbury, Malcolm. *The Modern American Novel.* New York: Penguin, 1994. Good survey by a British critic and comic novelist.

Bradbury, Malcolm, and James McFarlane, eds. *Modernism: 1890–1930.* Rev. ed. New York: Penguin, 1976. Includes essays on international aspects of modernism in the arts. A huge collection of essays, including an international chronology of events for the period.

Daiches, David. *The Present Age in British Literature.* Bloomington: Indiana UP, 1958. An influential though somewhat dated discussion, concentrating on the novel and poetry.

Eysteinsson, Astradur. *The Concept of Modernism.* Ithaca: Cornell UP, 1990. Excellent discussion of the relationship between modernism and modernity, with an international perspective.

Ford, Boris, ed. *The Modern Age.* 3rd ed. Baltimore: Penguin, 1973. Essays on backgrounds, literary movements, and authors.

Kenner, Hugh. *The Pound Era.* Berkeley: U of California P, 1971. A wide-ranging discussion centering on Pound's contribution to modernism.

Kenner, Hugh. *A Homemade World: The American Modernist Writers.* New York: Knopf, 1975. Discussions of poets and novelists, including longer discussions of Fitzgerald, Faulkner, and Hemingway.

Lee, Brian. *American Fiction, 1865–1940.* New York: Longman, 1987.

Nicholls, Peter. *Modernisms: A Literary Guide.* Berkeley: U of California P, 1995. An international perspective, stressing that literary modernism was made up of different conflicting political tendencies.

Stevenson, Randall. *Modernist Fiction: An Introduction.* Lexington: UP of Kentucky, 1992. Stresses modernist concepts of time and space.

Trotter, David. *The English Novel in History, 1895–1920.* New York: Routledge, 1993. Historical and social emphasis.

Wagner-Martin, Linda. *The Modern American Novel, 1914–1945: A Critical History.* Boston: Twayne, 1990.

There are in addition a multitude of excellent books focusing on a particular modernist decade, such as Frederic J. Hoffman, *The Twenties: American Writing in the Postwar Decade* (New York: Free, 1965), or on a novelistic technique, such as Melvin J. Friedman, *Stream of Consciousness: A Study in Literary Method* (New Haven: Yale UP, 1955), or on a subgenre, such as Mortimer R. Proctor, *The English University Novel* (Berkeley: U of California P, 1957). For others, consult the bibliographies of many of the books listed in this section.

3. FROM MODERNISM TO POSTMODERNISM

Bertens, Hans. *The Idea of the Postmodern: A History*. New York: Routledge, 1995. Concentrates on American sources in both literature and criticism.

Bradbury, Malcolm, ed. *The Novel Today: Contemporary Writers on Modern Fiction*. Totowa: Rowan, 1977. Reprints several well-known essays by Barth, Bellow, Fowles, Lodge, and Lessing, among others.

Calinescu, Matei. *Five Faces of Modernity: Modernism, Avant-Garde, Decadence, Kitsch, Postmodernism*. Durham: Duke UP, 1987. An attempt to situate modernist and postmodernist art within twentieth-century culture.

Connor, Steven. *The English Novel in History, 1950–1995*. New York: Routledge, 1996. A historical context for contemporary English fiction.

Dettmar, Kevin, ed. *Rereading the New: A Backward Glance at Modernism*. Ann Arbor: U of Michigan P, 1992. Revisionary essays on modernism in the light of postmodernism.

Elam, Diane. *Romancing the Postmodern*. London: Routledge, 1992. Argues for roots of the postmodern in the romance.

Fokkema, Douwe, and Hans Bertens, eds. *Approaching Postmodernism*. Amsterdam: Benjamins, 1986. Essays from a European perspective.

Foster, Hal, ed. *The Anti-Aesthetic: Essays on Postmodern Culture*. Port Townsend, WA: Bay, 1983. On art generally, with a theoretical emphasis.

Hassan, Ihab. *The Dismemberment of Orpheus: Toward a Post-Modern Literature*. 2nd ed. Madison: U of Wisconsin P, 1982. The leading American exponent of postmodernism.

Hutcheon, Linda. *A Poetics of Postmodernism: History, Theory, Fiction*. New York: Routledge, 1988. Develops concepts such as parody in the postmodern context.

Huyssen, Andreas. *After the Great Divide: Modernism, Mass Culture, Postmodernism*. Bloomington: Indiana UP, 1986. A very influential formulation in which popular culture is construed as modernism's feminine "other."

Jameson, Fredric. *Postmodernism, or, the Cultural Logic of Late Capitalism.* Durham: Duke UP, 1991. A theoretical Marxist perspective, paying attention to architecture and fine arts.

McHale, Brian. *Postmodern Fiction.* New York: Methuen, 1987. An influential attempt to define postmodernism in the novel.

Scholes, Robert. *Fabulation and Metafiction.* Urbana: U of Illinois P, 1979. An early celebration of what became postmodernism in fiction.

Sinfield, Alan. *Literature, Politics, and Culture in Postwar Britain.* Oxford: Blackwell, 1989.

Spilka, Mark, and Caroline McCracken-Flesher, eds. *Why the Novel Matters: A Postmodern Perplex.* Bloomington: Indiana UP, 1990. Essays on the state of the novel.

Waugh, Patricia. *Metafiction: The Theory and Practice of Self-Conscious Fiction.* New York: Methuen, 1984.

Waugh, Patricia. *Practicing Postmodernism/Reading Modernism.* London: Arnold, 1992.

Wilde, Alan. *Horizons of Assent: Modernism, Postmodernism, and the Ironic Imagination.* Baltimore: Johns Hopkins UP, 1981.

Writers at Work: The Paris Review Interviews. New York: Viking-Penguin. Valuable interviews with modern writers, published every few years from 1958 to 1988.

4. THE NOVEL, RACE, AND NATION

The African-American Novel

Baker, Houston A. *Blues, Ideology, and Afro-American Literature: A Vernacular Theory.* Chicago: U of Chicago P, 1984.

Baker, Houston A. *Modernism and the Harlem Renaissance.* Chicago: U of Chicago P, 1987.

Baker, Houston A. *Workings of the Spirit: The Poetics of Afro-American Women's Writing.* Chicago: U of Chicago P, 1990.

Carby, Hazel. *Reconstructing Womanhood: The Emergence of the Afro-American Woman Novelist.* New York: Oxford UP, 1987.

Christian, Barbara. *Black Women Novelists: The Development of a Tradition, 1892–1976.* Westpost: Greenwood, 1980.

Davis, Angela. *Women, Race, and Class.* New York: Vintage, 1993. Negotiates issues of feminism and social class as well as race.

Gates, Henry Louis, Jr., ed. *"Race," Writing, and Difference.* Chicago: U of Chicago P, 1986.

Gates, Henry Louis, Jr. *The Signifying Monkey: A Theory of African-American Literary Criticism.* New York: Oxford UP, 1988.

Jongh, James de. *Vicious Modernism: Black Harlem and the Literary Imagination.* Cambridge: Cambridge UP, 1990.

Morrison, Toni. *Playing in the Dark: Whiteness and the Literary Imagination.* Cambridge: Harvard UP, 1992.

North, Michael. *The Dialect of Modernism: Race, Language, and Twentieth-Century Literature.* New York: Oxford UP, 1994.

Stepto, Robert B. *From Behind the Veil: A Study of Afro-American Narrative.* 2nd ed. Urbana: U of Illinois P, 1991.

Werner, Craig Hansen. *Playing the Changes: From Afro-Modernism to the Jazz Impulse.* Urbana: U of Illinois P, 1994.

Postcolonial Writing

Ahmad, Aijaz. *In Theory: Nations, Classes, Literatures.* London: Verso, 1994. A leftist perspective.

Ashcroft, Bill, Gareth Griffith, and Helen Tiffin, eds. *The Empire Writes Back: Theory and Practice in Post-Colonial Literatures.* New York: Routledge, 1989. Inclusive survey of theory and criticism of world writing in English.

Ashcroft, Bill, Gareth Griffith, and Helen Tiffin, eds. *The Post-Colonial Studies Reader.* New York: Routledge, 1995. A good, inclusive collection of essays on broad topics. Over 500 pages.

Bhabha, Homi K. *The Location of Culture.* London: Routledge, 1994.

Bhabha, Homi K., ed. *Nation and Narration.* New York: Routledge, 1990. Sophisticated critical essays.

Eagleton, Terry, Fredric Jameson, and Edward W. Said. *Nationalism, Colonialism, and Literature.* Minneapolis: U of Minnesota P, 1990. Essays inspired by the Irish situation.

Said, Edward. *Culture and Imperialism.* New York: Knopf, 1993.

Spivak, Gayatri Chakravorty. *In Other Worlds: Essays in Cultural Politics.* New York: Routledge, 1988. Discusses critical theory, feminism, and the third world writing of India.

Williams, Patrick, and Laura Chrisman, eds. *Colonial Discourse and Post-Colonial Theory: A Reader.* New York: Columbia UP, 1994.

Young, Robert C. *Colonial Desire: Hybridity in Theory, Culture, and Race.* New York: Routledge, 1995.

Numerous other books address a specific cultural situation but may have broader relevance. See Ngugi wa Thiong'o, *Decolonising the Mind: The Politics of Language in African Literature* (London: Currey, 1986) and see the bibliographies in Ashcroft et al. and Williams.

5. GENDER CRITICISM

Feminism

Abel, Elizabeth, ed. *Writing and Sexual Difference*. Chicago: U of Chicago P, 1982.

Armstrong, Nancy. *Desire and Domestic Fiction: A Political History of the Novel*. New York: Oxford UP, 1987.

Benstock, Shari. *Textualizing the Feminine: On the Limits of Genre*. Norman: U of Oklahoma P, 1990.

Boone, Joseph, and Michael Cadden, eds. *Engendering Men: The Question of Male Feminist Criticism*. New York: Routledge, 1990.

Butler, Judith. *Gender Trouble: Feminism and the Subversion of Identity*. New York: Routledge, 1989. An influential theorist.

Davidson, Cathy. *Revolution and the Word: The Rise of the Novel in America*. New York: Oxford UP, 1986.

deKoven, Marianne. *Rich and Strange: Gender, History, Modernism*. Princeton: Princeton UP, 1991.

DuPlessis, Rachel Blau. *Writing beyond the Ending: Narrative Strategies of Twentieth-Century Writers*. Bloomington: Indiana UP, 1985.

Gilbert, Sandra, and Susan Gubar. *The Madwoman in the Attic: The Woman Writer and the Nineteenth-Century Literary Imagination*. New Haven: Yale UP, 1979.

Gilbert, Sandra, and Susan Gubar. *No Man's Land: The Place of the Woman Writer in the Twentieth Century*. Vol. 1, *The War of the Words*. New Haven: Yale UP, 1988. Vol. 2, *Sexchanges*. New Haven: Yale UP, 1988.

Marks, Elaine, and Isabel de Courtivron, eds. *New French Feminisms*. New York: Schocken, 1981.

Miles, Rosalind. *The Female Form: Women Writers and the Conquest of the Novel*. New York: Routledge, 1990.

Millett, Kate. *Sexual Politics*. Garden City: Doubleday, 1970.

Moers, Ellen. *Literary Women: The Great Writers*. New York: Doubleday, 1976.

Moi, Toril. *Sexual/Textual Politics: Feminist Literary Theory*. New York: Methuen, 1985.

Scott, Bonnie Kime. *Refiguring Modernism*. Bloomington: Indiana UP, 1995.

Scott, Bonnie Kime, ed. *The Gender of Modernism: A Critical Anthology*. Bloomington: Indiana UP, 1990.

Showalter, Elaine. *A Literature of Their Own: British Women Novelists from Brontë to Lessing*. Princeton: Princeton UP, 1977.

Spacks, Patricia Meyer. *The Female Imagination*. New York: Knopf, 1975.

Spender, Dale. *Mothers of the Novel: 100 Good Women Writers before Jane Austen*. New York: Pandora, 1986.

Todd, Janet. *Feminist Literary History*. New York: Routledge, 1988. An Anglo-American perspective.

Waugh, Patricia. *Feminine Fictions: Revisiting the Postmodern*. New York: Routledge, 1989. Suggests that the postmodern overlaps women's writing.

Gay and Lesbian Studies

Castle, Terry. *The Apparitional Lesbian: Female Homosexuality and Modern Culture*. New York: Columbia UP, 1993.

Dorn, Laura. *The Lesbian Postmodern*. New York: Columbia UP, 1994.

Farwal, Marilyn R. *Heterosexual Plots and Lesbian Narratives*. New York: New York UP, 1996.

Fuss, Diana, ed. *Inside/Out: Lesbian Theories, Gay Theories*. New York: Routledge, 1991.

Haggerty, George E., and Bonnie Zimmerman, eds. *Professions of Desire: Lesbian and Gay Studies in Literature*. New York: MLA, 1995. Includes a useful bibliography.

Jay, Karla, and Joanne Glasgow, eds. *Lesbian Texts and Contexts: Radical Revisions*. New York: New York UP, 1991.

Levin, James. *The Gay Novel in America*. New York: Garland, 1991.

Lilly, Mark. *Gay Men's Literature in the Twentieth Century*. New York: New York UP, 1993.

Meese, Elizabeth. *(Sem)erotics: Theorizing Lesbian Writing*. New York: New York UP, 1992.

Sedgwick, Eve Kosofsky. *Epistemology of the Closet*. Berkeley: U of California P, 1990. Perhaps the most influential theorist in gender studies.

Summers, Charles J. *Gay Fictions: Wilde to Stonewall, Studies in a Male Homosexual Literary Tradition*. New York: Continuum, 1990.

Zimmerman, Bonnie. *The Safe Sea of Women: Lesbian Fiction, 1969–1989*. Boston: Beacon, 1990.

GLOSSARY: ELEMENTS OF THE NOVEL

Because the glossary concentrates on terminology and the technicalities of narrative nomenclature, the following list features some major sources in narratology as well as books concentrating on plot, character, setting, and point of view. Forster, Scholes and Kellogg, Booth, and

Barthes, cited under chapter 1, are basic references. Bakhtin, also cited under chapter 1, lends a fresh linguistic perspective on character, setting, and point of view.

Bal, Miecke. *Narratology: Introduction to the Theory of Narrative*. Rev. ed. Trans. Christine van Boheemen. Toronto: U of Toronto P, 1985.

Brooks, Peter. *Reading for the Plot: Design and Intention in Narrative*. New York: Random, 1984. Freudian-influenced discussion with specific readings.

Chatman, Seymour. *Story and Discourse: Narrative Structure in Fiction and Film*. Ithaca: Cornell UP, 1978.

Cohan, Steven, and Linda M. Shires. *Telling Stories: A Theoretical Analysis of Narrative Fiction*. New York: Routledge, 1988. Clearly written synthesis, with concrete examples from fiction, comics, and film.

Cohn, Dorrit. *Transparent Minds: Narrative Modes for Presenting Consciousness in Fiction*. Princeton: Princeton UP, 1978.

Genette, Gérard. *Narrative Discourse: An Essay in Method*. Trans. Jane E. Lewin. Ithaca: Cornell UP, 1980.

Lanser, Susan Sniader. *The Narrative Act: Point of View in Prose Fiction*. Princeton: Princeton UP, 1981.

Martin, Wallace. *Recent Theories of Narrative*. Ithaca: Cornell UP, 1986. An excellent synthesis with a full bibliography.

Phelan, James. *Reading People, Reading Plots: Character, Progression, and the Interpretation of Narrative*. Chicago: U of Chicago P, 1989.

Phelan, James, ed. *Reading Narrative: Form, Ethics, Ideology*. Columbus: Ohio State UP, 1989. Good collection of essays focusing on the ethical implications of narration.

Price, Martin. *Forms of Life: Character and Moral Imagination in the Novel*. New Haven: Yale UP, 1983.

Rimmon-Kenan, Shlomith. *Narrative Fiction: Contemporary Poetics*. New York: Methuen, 1983.

Silverman, Kaja. *The Subject of Semiotics*. New York: Oxford UP, 1983. A Lacanian perspective.

Stevick, Philip, ed. *The Theory of the Novel*. New York: Macmillan, 1967. Excellent prestructuralist essays on narrative modes and forms.

ONLINE RESOURCES

An enormous amount of information, including graphics and sound clips as well as text, is available on the Internet and, for those with the proper browsers, on the World Wide Web. This material can be accessed through one of the search services, such as Lycos or Alta Vista, but it is most efficiently found through sites that offer annotated indexes of sites in a particular category.

Students should keep in mind that there is no guarantee of the accuracy of information on the Internet; however, sources attached to government institutions, universities, and major corporations are usually reasonably accurate. Another problem is that (unlike printed sources) sites can disappear, change their locations, or be radically transformed without warning. The following list is accurate as of this book's publication date.

1. Literary Resources on the Net (http://www.english.upenn.edu/~jlynch/lit) is a searchable page that also includes broad categories such as Twentieth-Century Irish and British Literature, American literature, Women's Literature and Feminism, and Ethnicities and Nationalities.

2. The Carnegie-Mellon English Server (http://english-server.hss.cmu.edu/) is an excellent resource with a great number of categories. It is especially strong in contemporary literary theory.

3. An Index of Web Sites on Modernism (http://www.modcult.brown.edu/people/Scholes/modlist/Title.html) is maintained by the Malcolm S. Forbes Center for Research in Culture and Media Studies at Brown University. It is a huge index of sites devoted to modernist art and artists, including cultural movements (such as the Harlem Renaissance), painters, and musicians, as well as writers. Artists are listed alphabetically; few strictly contemporary writers are included.

There are a host of web pages devoted to single authors, from James Joyce to Don DeLillo (http://haas.berkeley.edu/~gardner/delillo.html). From the James Joyce Resource Center (http://www.cohums.ohio-state.edu/english/organizations/ijjf/jrc/), for instance, you can reach online texts of Joyce's work, bibliographies and critical bibliographies, pages analyzing his works, and an online journal devoted to his writing, as well as over a dozen other Joyce sites.

Index

Edel, Leon, 19
Edgeworth, Maria, 95
Eggleston, Edward, 32
Eikhenbaum, Boris, 25
Einstein, Albert, 57, 58
eiron, 105
Eisenstein, Sergei, 54, 55
Eliot, George, 8, 10, 20, 95, 96, 110
Eliot, T. S., 20, 36, 37, 38, 39, 44, 45, 46, 47, 59, 64, 67
ellipsis, 113–14
Ellison, Ralph, 50, 69, 80, 81, 82, 86
Ellmann, Richard, 40
Emecheta, Buchi, 89
endomorph, 106
Engels, Friedrich, 40
entropy, 41
epic, 2, 109
epiphany, 18, 59, 114–15
episteme, 36
epistolary novel, 111
Erziehungsroman, 110
ethnic studies, 80
exempla, 2
exploration narrative, 22
exposition, 114
expressionism, 49–50

fables, 2
fabula, 113
falling action, 114
fantasy, 18, 123
Faulkner, William, 15, 17, 19, 36, 39, 45, 49, 54, 55, 58, 65, 67, 110, 112, 120, 121, 123
Fauset, Jessie, 47, 65
Feidelson, Charles, 40
feminism, 86, 93–99
Fern, Fanny, 99
fiction, novel as a form of, 1
Fiedler, Leslie, 70, 71, 74, 100–101

Fielding, Henry, 6–7, 18–19, 20, 22, 27, 106, 111
film, 52–56
Fisher, Dexter, 82
Fitzgerald, F. Scott, 17, 39, 55, 65, 121
flashback, 113
flashforward, 113
flat character, 18, 105
Flaubert, Gustave, 9, 12–13, 14, 15, 53, 117, 123–24
focalization, 120
Fokkema, Douwe, 75
folklore, 8, 9, 84, 107, 108
Ford, Ford Madox, 9, 15, 16, 18, 50, 64, 65, 66, 111, 113, 121
formalist criticism, 4–5, 24–25, 26
formal realism, 21
Forster, E. M., 18–19, 41–42, 64–65, 90, 100, 105, 113
Foucault, Michel, 28–29, 36, 75, 83, 90, 97, 98, 101
Fowles, John, 73, 76, 107, 119
Frame, Janet, 88
frame of reference, 58
Frank, Joseph, 58
Frazer, Sir James, 43–44
free verse, 50
Freud, Sigmund, 32, 36, 43, 52, 66, 89, 97, 116
Freytag, Gustav, 114
Freytag's triangle, 114
Fry, Roger, 35
Frye, Northrop, 23, 82, 115, 116
Fuentes, Carlos, 89
functions of characters, 108
Fussell, Paul, 37
futurism, 51

Galsworthy, John, 33, 64, 112
Galton, Francis, 35
Gandhi, Mohatma, 84
Gardner, Judith Kegan, 97
Garland, Hamlin, 64
Garnett, Edward, 17

Vertov, Dziga, 53, 54, 55
Victoria, Queen, 32, 35
Victorianism, 46, 119
vision, 120
Vivien, Renée, 101
Vizenor, Gerald, 75
voice, 120
Vonnegut, Kurt, Jr., 73
vorticism, 51–52

Wain, John, 70
Walcott, Derek, 89
Walker, Alice, 110
Walpole, Horace, 8, 111
Warner, Susan, 99
Warren, Robert Penn, 19, 68, 81
Washington, Booker T., 81
Watt, Ian, 21, 22, 23
Waugh, Evelyn, 67
Weber, Max, 35
Wells, H. G., 10, 33, 64
Welty, Eudora, 68
West, Nathanael, 52, 56, 74
Western Marxists, 26
Wharton, Edith, 64, 95
white diaspora, 88
White, Antonia, 96

White, Walter, 65
Whitman, Walt, 33, 100
Whittier, John Greenleaf, 32
Wilde, Oscar, 32, 88, 100
Wilder, Thornton, 50
Williams, Raymond, 20–21
Williams, William Carlos, 45, 48, 50, 51, 64
Winterson, Jeanette, 76
Wolfe, Thomas, 68
Woolf, Virginia, 15–16, 17, 18, 19, 20, 22, 35, 36, 37, 38, 39, 42, 45, 47, 48, 49, 50, 54, 59, 64, 66, 68, 93–94, 95, 96, 100, 106, 117
Wordsworth, William, 9, 59
World War I, 36–38
World War II, 68
Wright, Richard, 47, 67, 80, 82
Wylie, Philip, 56

Yeats, W. B., 39, 44, 88
Yonge, Charlotte, 99
Yorke, Henry, 68

Zimmerman, Bonnie, 100
Zola, Émile, 9, 14, 48–49, 106